Start Your Own

EVENT PLANNING BUSINESS

Additional titles in *Entrepreneur's* **Startup Series**

Start Your Own

Entrepreneur
MAGAZINE'S

start*up*

Start Your Own

2ND EDITION

EVENT
PLANNING
BUSINESS

Your Step-by-Step
Guide to Success

Entrepreneur Press and Amy Jean Peters

EP
Entrepreneur
Press

Editorial Director: Jere L. Calmes
Managing Editor: Marla Markman
Cover Design: Beth Hansen-Winter
Production and composition: Eliot House Productions

This publication is designed to provide accurate and authoritative information in regard to the subject matter covered. It is sold with the understanding that the publisher is not engaged in rendering legal, accounting or other professional services. If legal advice or other expert assistance is required, the services of a competent professional person should be sought.

Library of Congress Cataloging-in-Publication Data

ISBN-13: 978-1-59918-127-1 (alk. paper)
ISBN-10: 1-59918-127-4 (alk. paper)

Printed in United States

12 11 10 09 08 07   10 9 8 7 6 5 4 3 2

Contents

▲

Chapter 5

Financing Your Business 67

Chapter 6

The Fundamentals of Hiring Employees 79

Chapter 7

Marketing Your Business 91

Preface

Since *Start Your Own Event Planning Business* was first published in 2004, this field has blossomed. At the time of the first edition's printing, event planning had taken a bit of a downturn as the country was still reeling from 9/11 and coping with a less-than-robust economic picture.

Since 2004, though, the world of event planning has been one of growth and dynamism. A leading business magazine described event planning as one of the nation's "top jobs," ranking this fast-paced and energized career at No. 39. This same analysis predicted double digit growth for the field.

▲

This growth is fueled by robust economic news in many sectors. As companies thrive, they turn to event planners to hold myriad events every year. In fact, it is estimated that more than 1.2 million corporate events will be held in 2007 alone. This amazing number doesn't even factor in the millions of social events—birthday parties, weddings, bar and bat mitzvahs, anniversaries, reunions—which will be held during the same 12-month time frame.

Growth in the event planning industry also owes thanks to globalization. As companies create and develop global imprints with employees located at offices circling the earth, these businesses must periodically gather their employees for meetings and conferences. As globalization continues to expand, the demand for event planners to create and manage these global retreats will increase.

There also has been substantial growth in the number of events held by government agencies. Much of this growth has been spurred by post-9/11 response, focusing on bolstering homeland security.

Baby boomers are doing their part, too, increasing the demand for event planners. As the boomers age, they are holding ever more elaborate birthday parties and anniversaries, all of which are orchestrated by savvy event planners.

Event planning is a field that offers a wide array of career possibilities. Consider Lauren Polastri, owner of The Other Woman, an event planning business based in Connecticut. She has developed a thriving and sought-after part-time event planning business. Polastri created the company using a part-time model so she could be available for her young children.

On the other end of the spectrum is Susan Meyer, founder of Susan K. Meyer Consulting, a Washington-state-based event planning business specializing in high-touch social and corporate events. Meyer has planned hundreds of corporate and social events, from over-the-top, elaborate dinners for 12 to trade conferences with tens of thousands of attendees.

Cheryl Hagner represents another event-planning model. Director of University Events and Scheduling at Wesleyan University in Connecticut, Hagner and her staff oversee a staggering 9,000 events every year!

These varied models are another factor in the increasing attractiveness of the event-planning field. The field can accommodate anybody—from part- to full-time—who has the enthusiasm for developing a business in this always changing, always exciting business area.

The Event
Planning Industry

This book is a guide to developing a thriving business in this rapidly growing industry. It is an exciting time to throw your party hat into the event planning ring, as event planners are being called upon to develop and stage literally millions of events every year.

Event Planning News

For anyone thinking about developing a career in corporate event planning, the time is right. According to the most recent *Meetings Market Report*, a bi-annual source of information for planners, 90 percent of event planners anticipate holding the same number of events or more in the coming year, an indicator of the robust and growing state of this business field.

These events range from first-birthday parties to political fundraisers, anniversaries, bar and bat mitzvahs, fashion shows, product launches, conferences, graduations, and reunions, to name just a few!

According to a recent report in *The Wall Street Journal*, it takes about 150 hours for a planner, working with her staff, to produce a major event from start to finish. You do the math. Millions of events multiplied by 100's of hours spent planning equals many, many opportunities for those entering this field.

Yes, working in the field of event planning can mean long hours and high-stress moments— when the kitchen is accidentally set ablaze, for instance (something that Cheryl Hagner, Director of University Events and Scheduling at Wesleyan University, faced with aplomb). For the event planners interviewed in this guide, though, the rewards far outweigh any possible negatives. The field of event planning is fast-paced, creative, innovative, energizing, and offers the real possibility for earning big dollars.

This first chapter offers an overview, looking at what event planners do and why they do it. The chapter also includes an overview of the special events industry and a sampling of ideas for conducting your own market research, a must-do when creating a new business of any kind.

The Who, What, When, Where, and Why of Event Planning

We begin by considering the who, what, when, where, why, and how of event planning (although not in that order).

What Is Event Planning?

This question actually breaks down into two questions: What kinds of events are we talking about? What is event planning?

First, what kinds of events are we talking about? They include:

- *Celebrations* (fairs, parades, weddings, reunions, birthdays, anniversaries, bar and bat mitzvahs, first communions, sweet 16s)

- *Education* (conferences, conventions, meetings, graduations)
- *Promotions* (product launches, political rallies, fashion shows, conventions)
- *Commemorations* (memorials, civic events)

The above list is not an exhaustive one, but as the examples illustrate, special events may be business related, purely social, or somewhere in between. The advice in this book is relevant to the planning of both business and social events.

Now we move to the second What question: What is event planning?

Planners of an event may handle any or all of the following tasks related to that event:

- Conduct research
- Create an event design
- Find a site
- Arrange for food, decor, and entertainment
- Plan transportation to and from the event
- Send invitations to attendees
- Arrange any necessary accommodations for attendees
- Coordinate the activities of event personnel
  - Hire employees to work the event
- Supervise at the site
- Conduct evaluations of the event

How many of these activities your business engages in will depend on the size and type of a particular event, which will, in turn, depend on the specialization you choose. Your specialization will, of course, depend on your areas of expertise, but also will depend on your location. If you live in rural Iowa, for instance, you may be planning to develop a social event planning business since you may not have a strong corporate presence in your town.

When Do Event Planners Work?

Few event planners, if any, have 9-to-5 jobs (unless, of course, they have a day job and conduct their event planning as a sideline; this strategy may be a good one if you are just starting out). By its very nature, event planning tends to involve evenings, weekends, holidays, and sometimes even specific seasons. How much time, and when, you must commit to working will depend, once again, on the specialization you choose.

Deborah K. Williams estimates she works 60 to 65 hours per week. She, Kim Quigley, and David Granger are all stockholders in Designs Behind the Scenes, their 13-year-old event planning company in Dallas. Their business is a combination of corporate and private events and rentals. October is their busiest month for corporate events, followed by December. They have private events most weekends.

Industry expert John Daly points out that summer is a slow period for corporate events. Also, by the second week in December, all the corporate holiday events are over.

As a general rule, social events involve more weekends and holidays than corporate events. Some areas of the country and some types of events have on and off seasons. However, no matter what your specialization (with the exception of parties for young children), you can count on working at least some evenings as you coordinate and supervise events. The planning of those events, however, will be done mostly during business hours.

> **Tip...**
>
> **Smart Tip**
>
> It is vital that you consider your life and lifestyle as you plan a business in event planning. If you are raising young children, for instance, be sure that you have a system in place for reliable childcare. Nothing will sink your business faster, than if you are forced to miss events because your babysitter didn't show up as planned.

Where Do Event Planners Work?

Some event planners work out of their homes, while others rent office space for their businesses. Each of these strategies has advantages and disadvantages. Chapter 4 offers more advice on choosing the ideal location for your business.

Why Do People Hire Event Planners?

This question has a simple answer: Often individuals find that they lack the expertise and the time to plan events themselves. Independent planners can step in and give these events the attention they deserve.

Large businesses hire event planners to produce the myriad events—from golf tournaments to trade shows with tens of thousands of attendees—that are necessary each year.

Who Becomes an Event Planner?

Planners are often people who got their start in one particular aspect of special events.

Lauren Polastri, owner of The Other Woman, an event planning business based in Connecticut, laid the foundation for her business with a thriving catering business. Likewise, Martin Van Keken, of MVKA Productions in Vancouver, British Columbia, had a successful catering company before he decided to plan entire events. Initially,

Lee J. Howard Entertainment Inc. in Atlanta provided entertainment only. Then, in response to client requests, Howard branched out. Many other planners have similar stories. This explains why planners often not only coordinate entire events, but also may, in addition, provide one or more services for those events.

Often, owners of event planning businesses are also people who planned events for other companies before deciding to go into business for themselves. Joyce Barnes-Wolff planned in-house events for a retail chain for 11 years and then worked for another event planning company before starting JBW Productions in Columbus, Ohio. New York City planner Jaclyn Bernstein also planned events for another company before she and partner Robert Hulsmeyer bought it and turned it into Empire Force Events Inc.

Although the backgrounds of event planners may vary greatly, planners share many traits. Everyone we interviewed insisted that you have to have a passion for the event planning industry. Many said that they can't wait to get to the office most days. As industry expert Dr. Joe Goldblatt notes, "Successful event managers love their jobs."

John Daly, floral design specialist and industry expert, has written for industry publications, including *Special Events Magazine*. He also does a lot of public speaking. When he is asked about profits in the industry, he replies, "You have to get the passion, then the money will come. It's hard work. But it's rewarding if it's your passion."

Joyce Barnes-Wolff also stresses that people get into the event planning industry not because they want to get rich, but because they have a passion for it. "We all suffer from 'puppy syndrome,'" she says. "Clients love to throw us the ball and we'll run harder and faster every time they throw it and we'll jump over things. And all we want is for people to pat us on the head and say 'good job.'"

Barnes-Wolff has had many clients give her this figurative pat on the head. When she planned her first event, her task involved ". . .

putting on a pot of coffee and calling the press and trying to get 25 people to show up." She learned and grew along with the retail company she worked for, and her last event for that company was a shareholders meeting for 18,000 people. After that, she planned events for a production company for about five years before starting her own business, JBW Productions. Although her company is now seven years old, she did not initially intend to strike out on her own. "I was handed a chunk of business," she says. Her local convention visitors bureau hired her directly to produce the Capitol Lights event. Since she began her business, her company has expanded to produce other corporate and nonprofit events.

What about the personality of event planners? When asked what traits are important in the industry, planners listed the following:

- *Organizational ability.* Everyone mentioned this trait. Therefore, be warned: If you would rather count every blade of grass on your lawn than make a list, this profession is not for you.

Do You Have 'The Right Stuff'?

Event planners and industry experts have plenty of philosophies about their field and about their own roles in event planning. "Goodwill matters a lot in this business," says industry expert John Daly. "It's important to share knowledge." His motto? "Big fun is serious business."

"In this industry there is no right or wrong except to make the client happy," says David Granger.

Planners design events, hire personnel, and also contribute their own labor where needed. This multifaceted aspect of the profession explains Martin Van Keken's philosophy: "We're the architect, the contractor, and sometimes even the electrician," he says.

Joyce Barnes-Wolff views creative work as a major contribution her company makes to events. But creativity, she cautions, is not everything. "Without planning and follow-through, it's like a roof without a foundation," she says.

When asked about the qualities of successful event planners, Lee J. Howard has these succinct words: "Grace under pressure."

Jaclyn Bernstein knows exactly why event planners stick it out through pressure, crazy hours, and deadlines. "You have to love what you're doing," she says.

And, you may ask, what about a shared, industry-wide philosophy? Is there a motto? You bet. "You're only as good as your last event."

- *Attention to detail*. This is another must mentioned by most interviewees. Planners must think of, and keep track of, an amazing number of details. Planner Lee J. Howard suggests the following strategy, "Think from the completion of the result you want and then work backward to see how you can get there."

- *A stout heart*. You can't be faint-hearted and be a successful planner. You are in charge of the entire event, and there are no second chances.

- *Nerves of steel*. Glitches or no glitches, you must be upbeat and positive during the event. (You can cry and gnash your teeth later, in the car.)

- *Decision-making ability*. Anyone who is always the last of a group to order at a restaurant should consider a different industry. As an event planner, you will be called upon to make many decisions, sometimes in only a split second.

- *Good communication skills*. You'll need to convey your ideas and plans effectively to your clients, staff, and vendors, among others. You will need this ability not only as a sender, but also as a receiver of communication. Keep in mind that communication can be visual as well as verbal. Recognizing a blank look when you see one can enable you to clarify directions before some aspect of the event goes awry.

- *A liking for people*. This industry is very people-oriented. Jaclyn Bernstein mentioned a propensity for "taking care of people."

- *Creativity*. Whether you handle design elements of an event or not, creative talents are a definite plus. Furthermore, the definition of creativity may not always be what you think. "Creative is when you're on the job and Plan A isn't going to work and you have half an hour to figure out Plan B," says Patty Sachs, author of *Pick a Party Cookbook: The Big Book of Theme Party Refreshments and Table Décor*, among other books.

- *Flexibility*. "There's always something that will go differently than planned," says Martin Van Keken. "You've got to be ready. And you've got to be able to think on your feet."

- *Tact*. Sometimes you will have to break unhappy news to clients. For example, their budgets may not always be big enough to accomplish what they want. Also, they may want decor elements that either will not work well or are inappropriate. While these problems are less common when dealing with corporate clients, you will still find tact a necessary ingredient in successful business relationships.

> **Tip...**
>
> **Smart Tip**
> If you decide to volunteer, make sure you are not an "invisible" volunteer, one of the masses. Make sure you are assisting the person in charge and that you get experience with a large variety of tasks.

If you have most of these traits, event planning may be a good profession for you. How do you find out for sure? "Volunteer, volunteer, volunteer!" says Sachs. "Offer to assist the chairperson of a large fundraising event, the bigger the better. Follow that person through from start to finish, sitting in on all meetings and pushing the event over the hill, grunt work included. This will establish the area of planning that you find most appealing and for which you are most suited." If you already have some idea of which types of events you'd like to plan, make sure you concentrate your volunteer efforts there.

Tip...

Smart Tip

Depending on the type of services they offer, independent planners might call themselves by any of the following titles: program manager, project manager, event planner, principal executive, fundraising consultant, development consultant, meeting consultant, or event coordinator, among others.

How Do Event Planners Do It?

The answer to this question is what this book, as well as your own experience, will show you. So pull up a comfortable chair and read on. Our first step will be to examine the event planning industry itself.

A History Lesson

The special events industry has grown enormously in the last two decades. According to recent research conducted by Dr. Joe Goldblatt, Certified Special Events Professional (CSEP), annual spending for special events worldwide is estimated at $500 billion. Goldblatt is the founder of International Special Events Society (ISES) and the founding director of the Event Management Program at George Washington University. Currently at Johnson and Wales University, he is the dean of the Alan Shawn Feinstein Graduate School, which offers the first MBA concentration in Event Leadership.

According to U.S. government census information, job growth in this field is on the uptick. Globalization has added to this surge as these multi-national businesses call on event planners to develop meetings for their globetrotting staffs. These companies recognize that only so much work can be conducted via phone and e-mail (remember the deals that are made on the golf course when business associates come -to-face!). Ultimately, the players in these large corporations need to come :ther in one place. This is when the event planner is called into play.

Studies show that the average event planner now earns about $60,000, with plenty of room for growth to this already healthy income.

Goldblatt adds that the social events market is booming. "As the baby boomers age, they have more to celebrate—and do!" He points out that a record number of Americans are turning 50 in the next few years—and they will mark their birthdays with flashy events.

Sachs agrees, "The event, party, and celebration industry is growing more each year, in a steady way." Like Goldblatt, she points out the large number of baby boomers celebrating milestone birthdays. In addition, she says, many are now celebrating landmark anniversaries or their offsprings' graduations and weddings. "To top all of this, these baby boomers are often owners or executives in businesses that were established some 25 years ago, which brings about many corporate celebrations."

Also booming is the children's birthday party business, with over-the-top first birthday celebrations and extravagant sweet 16s contributing to the rapid growth of this aspect of event planning.

Although potential profits, especially in social event planning, are substantial, keep in mind that it takes the average event planning business two to three years to make a healthy profit. Why? One reason is that most clients come from word-of-mouth referrals, and it can take a while before a solid base of contacts is developed. More about building a solid client base will be covered in Chapter 7.

> ## Bright Idea
>
> When a company holds a meeting in a major city and the attendees travel to the meeting from other cities or states, a planner may use a destination manager's services to take care of the attendees' needs at their meeting location. Destination managers coordinate and supervise meetings in their cities, transport attendees to and from their hotels and airports, and take attendees on tours to give them a feel for the cities they are visiting. Jaclyn Bernstein, president of Empire Force Events Inc. in New York City, handles a lot of destination management business.

A Sophisticated Turn

Along with increased demand for special events, and perhaps because of it, the industry has become much more sophisticated. According to Daly, "It's become a force to be reckoned with." Twenty years ago, he says, a party was a tablecloth and a centerpiece. Event planners were not taken seriously. When he told people he created parties for a living, he remembers, it was laughable. "Now it's interesting," he says.

David Granger, a veteran in the industry, concurs. "People know what they are looking for," he says. "A certain quality is expected now."

Joyce Barnes-Wolff makes a similar point: "There is more credibility than . . . when event specialists were the people who did country club parties." Now, she adds, huge concerns like Disney, Radio City Music Hall, Universal Studios, Paramount, and others have become involved in the special events industry.

Who Hires Event Planners

Broadly speaking, there are two markets for event planning services: corporate and social. Market information is more readily available for corporate meetings than for other events, but we will attempt to give you a good idea of both markets.

The Corporate Market

We will use the term corporate to include not only companies but also charities and nonprofit organizations. All these entities use special events to reach their target markets and to increase their visibility in the community. In fact, special events have become increasingly important as competition forces organizations to look for new ways to get their messages across to consumers or contributors.

Charities and nonprofit organizations host gala fundraisers, receptions, and athletic competitions, among other events, to expand their public support base and raise the funds they require. Such organizations find that special events are cost-effective and have a high impact. Thousands of these events occur each year, and although the large ones require specialized event planning experience, you may find smaller local events to plan.

Companies host trade shows, conventions, company picnics, holiday parties, and meetings for staff members, board members, or stockholders. There is a huge market for these types of events. In one year alone, the total number of meetings held in the United States is well over 1 million, according to *Meetings Market Report* conducted for *Meetings & Conventions* magazine.

Whether you plan meetings, fundraisers, or receptions, there are opportunities available in corporate event planning.

Patty Sachs, author of party-planning books and newsletters, says that corporations want events that are original and striking enough to be long remembered: "Themes are extremely popular." Lauren Polastri, of The Other Woman has also found that her clients are asking for more event-themed parties and events. Unusual customized entertainment, and an increased degree of guest involvement are gaining in popularity. The bottom line for most party givers—corporate or

Stat Fact

The *Meetings Market Report* is conducted every two years and published in *Meetings & Conventions* magazine, a leading source for the meetings industry.

social—is that they want to feel that their party was special or unique in some way.

Planning corporate events can provide you with a steady, profitable amount of business, but if you are a beginning event planner, Daly recommends that you begin by planning social events.

The Social Market

Social events include weddings, birthdays, anniversary parties, bar and bat mitzvahs, Sweet 16 parties, children's parties, reunions, etc. You may decide to handle all these events or to specialize in one or more of them.

Most people who employ event planners for these types of parties are in the middle- to upper-income levels and have some spare income but no spare time. Such clients are likely to live in affluent suburbs. Typically, these clients have household incomes of at least $60,000.

The market for social events, especially birthdays and anniversaries, is expected to continue to increase over the next few years, as baby boomers mature. This group has children getting married, parents celebrating golden anniversaries, and their own silver wedding anniversaries to celebrate. Industry experts agree that baby boomers will be a major source of income for event planning entrepreneurs in the coming years.

Conducting Market Research

Many interviewees told us that their market research was very informal in nature, consisting of knowledge gained through years of involvement in the industry. Deborah Williams, Kim Quigley, and David Granger all have years of experience in the event planning or supply industry. Their target market is the Dallas-Ft. Worth area. However, they also operate nationally, producing corporate events in Florida, Oklahoma, and Ohio. Most of their clients come to them through organizations they belong to or because they have been involved in the industry for many years. "So you know the resources and the people," Quigley says.

If you already have experience in event planning or a related industry, you may be starting your own business partly because discussions with colleagues make you aware that a need exists. This kind of knowledge is valuable, but Goldblatt points out that competition is now global as well as local, and all event planners should do market research. With this idea in mind, we now offer some suggestions on how to conduct this type of research.

The Market Analysis

One of your first tasks is to determine the market limits or trading area of your business. These limits will vary depending upon the type of event planning service you offer. For example, if you plan parties, you may limit your market to your county. If you plan corporate meetings, however, you may have a national client base.

Studies show that a population base of at least 50,000 is needed to support an event planning service. Keep in mind that the higher the income level of that population, the more potential clients there will be for your business.

If you live in an area with a population base of less than 50,000, consider your goals. Perhaps, you are a mother of young children and are hoping to earn $5,000 a year, keeping your business small while rearing your children. Then, a smaller population base may work for you. Many event planners put their hats into this business, planning to earn only a part-time salary to supplement other family income. This is one of the real strengths of this field. You can choose to create a successful part-time or full-time business in event planning.

To conduct a market analysis you need to ask and answer to the following questions:

- Is the population base large enough to support your event planning service?
- Does the community have a stable economic base that will provide a healthy environment for your business?
- Are the area's demographic characteristics compatible with the market you wish to serve?

Many chambers of commerce have offices that track their area's economic development. These offices are usually called either Office of Economic Development or Economic Development Council. Find an office in your area, and look for the above information. In addition, look at reports and studies conducted by trade associations. You can also contact the Census Bureau at www.census.gov.

You can also access www.bls.gov/cex/ to read the Bureau of Labor's Consumer Expenditure Survey. This survey includes information about how individuals and families spend their money.

If you'll be planning corporate events, you also need to know the number of corporations in your service area that hold regular conventions and meetings, the size of these companies, their budgets for these events, and if they are using outside services. You will be able to find answers to many of these questions on a company's web site.

As you conduct your market research, memberships in industry-related associations can be well worth the investment. Associations usually offer networking opportunities and a wealth of industry-specific information, such as market statistics, ⸱r lists, books, and reference materials. They may also offer discounts on pur- from certain suppliers.

There are several associations specific to the event planning industry, including the International Special Events Society and Meeting Professionals International. For information on contacting an industry association, please see the Appendix at the end of this guide.

Interview Prospective Clients

The next step is to interview prospective clients. What are their needs? How likely are they to use a service like yours? If you are planning corporate events, interview meeting planners and directors of marketing and public relations, as well as event directors at convention halls and hotels. If your business will focus on social events, interview women in affluent households (studies show women do most social planning). Whatever your specialization, also consider interviewing professionals in related fields. Photographers and caterers know a lot about the nature of the special events occurring in the area. You can survey your targeted market by direct mail, by telephone, by e-mail, or in person.

Next, Goldblatt suggests, try to get a few clients. "If people are not willing to pay you, they're not fully committed," he says.

Analyze the Competition

Competition in the event planning market is fierce, but it is not insurmountable. If you are targeting the corporate market, your competition will consist not only of other event planning entrepreneurs, but also of in-house meeting planners hired by corporations. Many corporations choose to outsource event planning responsibilities to keep costs low. You may be able to assess the competition by asking corporations about the planners they work with. Trade associations such as ISES or MPI may not be able to disclose members' names, but they might be willing to tell you how many of their members are located in your area.

In the social arena, your main competition will be other event planning entrepreneurs, as well as some caterers, florists, etc., who have taken on the responsibilities of planning events as a sideline function. Most of the competition you'll face will be local; try checking in your phone book under Event Planners or Party Planners to see how many others there are. Be aware, however, that many event planners do not buy advertising, preferring to rely solely on

Dollar Stretcher

Check with area colleges and universities for free assistance in conducting your market research. Many schools will give credit to business students for helping you to do your market research. They receive college credit, you receive valuable information, and everyone is happy!

Profile

Dallas planner Kim Quigley says she spends most of her time on vendor consultations, networking, bookkeeping, and event design. However, she also conducts on-site supervision, consults with clients, and routes deliveries to event venues. She goes to staff meetings once a week and travels about three

word-of-mouth to do their advertising for them. This means you may have to get creative to figure out how much local competition you face. Ask vendors which planners they work with. Go to party supply stores and see if you can find out who their major customers are. Ask all your questions face-to-face, rather than by phone. If you are friendly and explain that you are trying to figure out if there is enough demand for another planning business, most people will cooperate.

If you find a large amount of competition in your area, don't be discouraged. Instead, look for a niche you can fill and think about what will make your event planning company stand out in the crowd. Social event planning is the ideal place from which to launch your career. Social planning is a growth industry—there are more opportunities out there than those planners in the marketplace can handle. Social event planners also will be able to find plenty of work in areas with a smaller population base.

Remember that if you strive to be the best, research your market, promote yourself, and develop a good business plan, you *will* find your spot in the marketplace.

Building Your Business Foundation

Now that you've decided to pursue a career in event planning, it is time to build a solid foundation upon which to build your business. Before you plan your first event, you will need to research the industry, find your niche, determine start-up costs, and create a plan for business success.

Industry Research

Some aspects of event planning are much more complicated than many entrepreneurs realize. The delicacies of developing solid vendor relations, establishing good rapport with clients, and heading off potential problems before they affect your event (and therefore your reputation) can only be conquered by study and experience.

Even so, your research shouldn't stop here. You should also do the following:

- *Conduct the market research as outlined in Chapter 1.* There is no substitute for doing your homework.

- *Network with other event planning entrepreneurs and business owners by joining local associations.* Industry ties are crucial in the event planning business.

- *Contact the national associations for the latest in research and practice guidelines, as well as for any other help they can provide.* You can find the relevant contact information in the Appendix.

- *Keep up with industry trends through business journals and other publications.* These are valuable resources.

- *Read everything you can find on the event planning industry.* This includes newspaper features and articles in glossy magazines like *Vanity Fair* and *Town & Country*, which chronicle the parties of the rich and powerful. Reading these glossies will help you to keep on top of trends, essential in this business.

- *Volunteer your time to a local charity event.* Not only will you get hands-on experience, but also you'll make valuable contacts that will help you down the road. Be an effective volunteer—not a wallflower. Make your presence known to the organizer of the event.

Event Planning News

Event planners interviewed for this guide point out that the field of event planning has become increasingly complex, as consumer tastes become more sophisticated and more elaborate events are staged. Because of this growing complexity, it is becoming increasingly common for event planners to earn a bachelor's degree, according to U.S. Census information. Degrees in marketing, communications, and business are useful to event planners as they develop their businesses. Remember, though, that a degree is not required and, as event planners point out, degree or no degree, nothing beats real, in-the-trenches event planning experience.

Finding Your Niche

ve already mentioned the fact that most event professionals focus on either ate or social events. However, you should consider specializing even further,

Making the Grade

Consider getting a degree or certificate from a local university in event planning or management. According to industry expert Dr. Joe Goldblatt, 300 colleges and universities offer classes in event management. A list of the institutions offering educational opportunities in this field is available from Meeting Professionals International (MPI). (See the Appendix for contact information.)

Also consider working to become a Certified Special Events Professional (CSEP) or Certified Meeting Planner (CMP). These designations are given out by International Special Events Society (ISES) and MPI, respectively. Many corporations, and some members of the general public, look for these designations when hiring planners. Because of the research and study it takes to become a CMP or CSEP, clients know that these planners are professionals.

---

narrowing your attention to children's parties, corporate retreats, or other types of events. Why? "Without a niche market, it makes it hard for the market to find you," says Dr. Joe Goldblatt, industry expert and founder of ISES. For example, if you're known as your community's expert on anniversary parties, a client wanting to throw such a party is more likely to come to you than to a general party planner.

Specializing in one or two types of events will also make your job easier. You can become an expert in one type of event faster than you can in multiple events. Specializing will save you time because you'll soon be familiar with all the elements of, and vendors required for, the type of event you choose. And as an event professional, time is one of your most valuable resources—the more you can save, the better.

Profile

Event planner David Granger handles a variety of events, both corporate and social. Recently he has expanded his services to include bar and bat mitzvahs. However, he has many years of experience with large events. "I do dinner parties and events for hotels, with buffet tables, special effects, and entertainment."

Selecting a niche will also help you to save on start-up costs since you will need to buy supplies only relevant to your specialization. For instance, if you choose children's birthday party planning as your niche, you won't need to buy complicated event-planning software designed for larger events.

Choosing a Specialty

Industry expert, consultant, and author Patty Sachs agrees that specializing is a good way to establish yourself in the industry. She suggests the following possible niches for social event planners:

- Hospitality suites (events held in the "party" room of a retirement home or a business)
- Parties away from home (events hosted by hotel guests)
- Surprise parties
- Progressive parties (events at more than one venue, usually involving transportation from one location to another—e.g., tours, scavenger hunts)
- His 'n' hers showers (wedding and baby)
- Birthday parties for 1-year-olds
- Theme parties
- "Golden" parties (50th anniversaries, 50th birthdays, etc.)
- Milestone birthdays
- Weekend event guest services (events to entertain out-of-town guests over the weekend—e.g., tours, barbecues)
- Kids' parties
- Kids' event areas for grown-up parties

The niches listed above all have a social focus, even though your client might also be a corporation. Below we list some additional possibilities for finding your niche in business-related events.

- Mall events (fashion shows, store grand openings, department-store promotions)
- Meetings and conferences
- Awards events
- Fundraisers
- Corporate retreats or picnics

If you do decide to focus on one type of event, be sure that your market area has enough of a demand, as discussed in Chapter 1. If you live in a rural area, developing a business based on organizing corporate meetings and conferences is probably not as sensible—

Profile

Industry expert John Daly, CSEP, started his first event planning company in the mid-'70s on $4,000. He drove an old van, which he parked out of sight. His first location was a 250-square-foot workroom in Los Angeles. He spent the majority of his start-up money on two suits. "I wanted to look successful," he explains. "It worked." Within four years he had 35 full-time employees and a fleet of cars. "I was at the right place at the right time."

Bright Idea

Lauren Polastri, owner of The Other Woman, reports that parties with South of the Border flare are hot right now. "The theme makes an event, and this party theme is very in. My clients like the colors and the tastes that are associated with Mexico and Latin and South America."

or as profitable—as developing an event planning business focusing on social events.

Calculating Start-Up Costs

How much money will you need to start your event planning business? That will depend on the cost of living in the area your business serves and whether you work from home or rent office space. It will also depend on your own taste and lifestyle choices.

Keep in mind that while working from home will keep your costs low, you must still buy equipment and a good insurance policy. You may also need advertising, although many event planners rely solely on word of mouth advertising.

Special Delivery

Most planners we interviewed specialized in either social or corporate events, with little mixing of the two types. Which of these you choose (or whether you choose to mix them) will depend on several factors:

○ *Amount of experience*. Industry expert John Daly points out that corporations are extremely sophisticated. If you are just starting out in the industry, he recommends beginning with private events. "You have to get seasoned before you do corporate events."

○ *Personality*. Clients tend to have more invested, emotionally, in social events. Generally speaking, social event planning requires even greater degrees of patience and tact than does corporate event planning.

○ *Lifestyle preference*. Consider what you expect as time off and whether you have strong feelings about the time of year you'd like to vacation. Everyone interviewed mentioned that they work long hours, well over 40 per week. "Private parties take a lot more time than corporate events. They're much more demanding," says Daly. This is partly because of the client's emotional investment in the event. Working during holidays is a virtual certainty if you do social parties. Furthermore, specializing in wedding anniversary parties might have you heavily booked in the spring and gasping for work the rest of the year. Planning children's birthday parties will, in most cases, leave your evenings free. A corporate specialization, on the other hand, may involve more travel.

All these expenses can be costly. The start-up worksheet below will help to give you an indication of how much money you will need to start your event planning service. Fill in the column labeled "My Own" with your own estimated costs.

This chart lists the start-up costs for two hypothetical event planning services. The first business is homebased with no permanent employees. The owner already has a basic computer and modem and some office furniture. She used her start-up money to buy liability insurance, event-planning software, a better cell phone, a digital camera, and a multifunction printer/copier/fax machine. She also established a web site and paid a graphic design student to produce a high-quality business card and letterhead logo. She started her business on a shoestring.

The higher end business occupies 1,000 square feet of office space. The owner/manager of this business employs a full-time junior planner and a part-time bookkeeper, as well as temporary employees who handle clerical work and who may help prepare for various events. This owner upgraded her existing computer equipment, bought office furniture and cell phones for herself and her assistant, added a phone line and a web site, bought several types of insurance, and invested in business cards, stationery, and an ad in the Yellow Pages.

Start-Up Expenses

Start-Up Expenses	Low	High	My Own
Rent/security deposit	$0	$2,300	
Equipment	$5,000	$17,000	
Inventory	$0	$500	
Licenses and taxes	$250	$350	
Communications	$100	$250	
Payroll	$0	$4,000	
Advertising/promotion	$500	$2,000	
Legal fees and accounting	$650	$1,500	
Insurance (first quarter)	$800	$1,700	
Miscellaneous	$750	$1,500	
Total	$8,050	$31,1000	

Stat Fact
A thorough business plan tends to be about 25 pages long and involve 300 hours of preparation. Plan on writing this plan yourself rather than hiring a writer because you want the plan to reflect your voice and personal vision of your company. If you are not secure in your role as writer, have a free-lance editor look over your finished plan for polishing any stylistic or grammatical issues.

Both owners will derive their income from pre-tax net profit. Annually, these new businesses will gross $85,000 and $250,000, respectively. The start-up table lists pre-opening costs for the businesses.

Creating a Map for Success

To make sure you keep your business goals and strategies clearly in sight, you need a well organized and thoughtfully drafted business plan as well as a succinct and convincing mission statement.

Your Business Plan

Broadly speaking, your business plan should discuss the event planning industry, your business structure, the service you will offer, your clients, the competition and how you will beat it, your income and cash flow, and other relevant financial information.

A well-conceived business plan will provide you with a map for the future of your venture, as well as something by which to gauge your progress. Your plan thus becomes an operating tool that will help you manage your business. In addition, a business plan is the chief instrument you will use to communicate your ideas to others—including business people, bankers, and partners. If you seek financing for your business, the plan will become the basis for your loan proposal. Even if you don't plan to seek financing, you must take the time to write a business plan. This plan will help you to cement the logistics and growth curve of your new business.

The Components of a Successful Business Plan

Every thorough and useful business plan should contain the following seven components:

- *Executive summary*. As the name suggests, this section summarizes your entire business plan. It includes details about the nature of your business, the type and scope of event planning services that you will provide, the legal form of your business (covered in Chapter 4), and your vision and goals for the business.

- *Business description.* In this section you'll describe the event planning business as a whole and your target market. Use specifics here, hard numbers, and facts. Along with those found in this guide, you'll find more event planning statistics at uscensus.gov.

- *Market strategies.* Here you will describe exactly how you will reach out to and market to prospective clients. Again, be as specific as possible. Will you advertise in the Yellow Pages? Join professional organizations for networking? Use newsletters as a marketing device? Include as many of these details as possible. Also, take time in this section to write about the ways in which your company is unique and, therefore, better than your competitors.

- *Competitive analysis.* In this section, focus on likely competitors in your field. Discuss how your services will differ from other event planners. Also, don't forget to focus on other potential competitors, such as hotels and banquet halls with inhouse staffs to plan events. Why are your services preferable to those of your competitors? It is essential that you clearly formulate the ways in which your company will differentiate itself from competitors.

- *Design and development plan.* This is an opportunity to discuss how you will develop markets for your business and develop an ever broader client base. Set specific goals. Perhaps you plan to develop and hold ten social events during your first year of business and to grow that number to 25 events per year by your fifth year in the event planning business.

- *Operations and management plan.* How will you run your business on a day-to-day basis? Will this be a part- or full-time career for you? Will you hire employees? Consider a typical day in your business and describe it here and how you will facilitate this operation.

- *Financial factors.* This is the section in which to focus on your financial expectations. Even if you are opening the business as a very part-time occupation—for instance, planning only five events per

> **⚠ Beware!**
> You may be tempted to forgo creating and writing a business plan. Don't give in to this temptation. Ask any successful business owner and she will tell you that the business plan was key to her success. A business plan helps you to envision and plan your business and is absolutely vital if you plan to seek financing.

> **Profile**
> Deborah Williams says she and Kim Quigley spent $5,000 in 1990 to start Designs Behind the Scenes. They bought basic office equipment, including a computer and fax machine. They also invested in distinctive, high-quality business cards.

On a Mission

When writing a mission statement, consider these tips:

❍ *Keep it brief.* One or two sentences is ideal. Never write a mission statement longer than four sentences.

❍ *Answer the who, what, and why of your company.* Tell who your company is, what you do and what you stand for, and tell why you do it and why you have a passion for it.

❍ *Look at other mission statements.* Choose a company you admire and visit its web site to read the mission statement.

❍ *Don't write a hyperbolic mission statement.* Write a mission statement in which you can truly believe.

year—you will need to forecast your financial future. Consider where you would like to be financially in one year and in five years and include that information here.

Crafting a Mission Statement

Your mission statement also plays a crucial role in giving your business every chance for success. Quite simply, a mission statement identifies, in as little as one sentence, your company's goals.

Consider the power of athletic giant Nike's mission statement: "To bring inspiration and innovation to every athlete* in the world. *If you have a body, you are an athlete." These two carefully crafted sentences give a world of information about Nike and its vision.

One way in which to consider your mission statement is to view it as a cross between a slogan and a corporate summary. As with your business plan, take time to carefully consider this statement. Make sure that you are able to remember your mission statement—if you can't remember it, then no one else will be able to either!

3

A Day in
the Life

This chapter covers the nuts and bolts of plan-

ning an event, outlining the steps involved, and giving helpful

hints.

Dr. Joe Goldblatt, CSEP, has identified what he calls

the Five Phases of Event Management: research, design, planning,

coordination, and evaluation. His focus is on the production of

Event Planning News

According to the most recent *Convention Center Report*, produced by Pricewaterhouse Coopers, convention center occupancy rates are on the uptick. The report also notes that centers of all size are experiencing robust growth, good news for event planners.

large-scale events, and he has written several books on the topic (see the Appendix). Here we borrow his framework and adapt it to include the production of smaller events, with one vocabulary change. Because we use the term planning in this book to talk about the overall activity that includes these five phases, we will avoid confusion by referring to this phase as organization.

Research

The best way to reduce risk (whatever the kind) is to do your homework. For large events, research may mean making sure that there is a demand for the event. To find out this kind of information, you can conduct surveys or interviews, or you can assemble small groups of potential attendees, called focus groups, for discussion. Although you are researching demand for an event instead of demand for your business, the strategies are the same as those discussed in the market research sections in Chapter 1.

The Essentials

Susan Meyer, owner and founder of Susan K. Meyer Consulting, says that successful event planners must have:

- ○ *Excellent oversight of a project as a whole.* As Meyer points out, event planning is challenging in that successful event planners must have both big-picture and small-picture abilities. In other words, while planning an event for thousands and conceiving an overarching design, she must also manage literally hundreds of details.
- ○ *Astute time-line management abilities.* Event planners must coordinate dozens and dozens of details which must all come together at the right time. One missed cue—for instance, the DJ who shows up late—can crash the party.
- ○ *Vendor negotiation skills.* Meyer uses these skills to negotiate money-saving deals for her clients.

Profile

Lauren Polastri, of The Other Woman event planning service, has found event planning a perfect career while raising young children. "I love my work because it allows me to work around my kids' schedules. Through the grace of nice people, my business has blossomed. I am a newly single mom so it has been very important that my business schedule accommodates my family life."

Research can take different forms. For instance, if you are planning an event that will be held in another city, the local convention and visitors bureau should be able to help you. It can guide you to a hotel that meets your client's needs and stays within your budget. These bureaus should also have a great deal of information on local attractions and sites for meetings and conventions. Convention personnel in hotels can offer valuable suggestions, but remember that they may have their own agendas. If you intend to look for suppliers or vendors in a city you have never visited, ask for referrals from other planners who have worked there. They may be able to direct you to excellent providers.

If you are new to the event planning industry, research may mean finding out all you can about vendors and suppliers. As you meet with potential vendors, note which events they specialize in and how much they charge. Even if you decide during the interview that you won't use their services right away, you should still take notes for future reference. Industry expert, author, and consultant Patty Sachs recommends using small cards and filing them in a box divided into main-event supplier categories. She cautions owners to note prices, style numbers, lead time, contact persons, and anything else that seems pertinent, even if you don't use the vendor for that particular event. "You are as good as your Rolodex," she advises. You could also list this information on your computer if you prefer. For more information on hiring vendors, see Chapter 6.

Research also may mean talking to other planners who have produced events similar to the one on which you are working. Or you may find yourself reading up on issues of custom and etiquette, especially if you are unfamiliar with a particular type of event.

Whatever kind of event you are planning, research should include asking your client a lot of questions and writing down the answers. New York City planner Jaclyn Bernstein, Destination Management Certified Professional (DMCP), works primarily with clients from out of town.

Smart Tip

Tip...

All of the event planners interviewed for this book agree that word of mouth is tbe ideal way in which to find the best vendors. Ask other event planners, as well as those who have recently held events, to recommend vendors. It's likely you'll find the same vendor names coming up time and time again.

Profile

Joyce Barnes-Wolff of JBW Productions in Ohio keeps a drawer of new ideas. "Look at movies, music, what people are doing, what's hot." Wherever she goes and whatever she's doing, one little corner of her mind is always idea-gathering. "I can't shut it off," she says.

To avoid communication problems, she makes sure she knows what the client's goals are and how the client thinks the event should be handled. "Try to use the client's exact words in your proposal," she suggests.

Always find out what customers hope to accomplish with an event. Do they want to introduce a new product, motivate employees, or provide a forum for networking? Do they want to put together a spectacular college reunion? Do they want to celebrate their parents' anniversary with an unforgettable party? Clients may want an event that is strictly business, strictly social, or somewhere in between.

Interviewing a client may not be what you immediately think of as research. However, asking too few questions or not listening adequately to a client's answers can compromise the success of the event you plan. Also, be sure to ask the right type of questions, questions that allow the respondents to clearly express their preferences. Questions with simple "yes" or "no" answers will tend to be less helpful to your planning process.

When planning, you'll need to garner the following information:

- *Who?* Who are the attendees, and how many of them will be at the event (a dozen company executives, 30 children, 80 elderly ping-pong enthusiasts)?
- *What?* What kind of event will this be (a family reunion, an elegant sit-down banquet, a fashionable but laid-back art show reception)? Don't forget to ask about the style of the event (formal, relaxed, traditional, avant garde, etc.), and whether your client wants a theme event (see discussion below).
- *When?* Find out the date of the event.
- *Where?* The client may want you to suggest a venue for the event, but you should always find out what type of location is desired (something unusual, informal, elegant? indoors or outdoors?).
- *Why?* Find out the reason for the event. What is the client's goal or objective?
- *How?* How does the client want guests to remember the event? As the most original picnic they've ever been to? As a holiday evening filled with one surprise after another? As a company party with the best food they've had in a long time? The issue of how guests should remember an occasion is crucial in deciding which aspects of the event should be given priority. Recognizing that few clients have unlimited funds, always find out what aspects of the event your customer feels are most important.

By Invitation Only

Any invitations you send potential attendees should include the following information:

- ○ Event
- ○ Host's name
- ○ Date
- ○ Time
- ○ Location
- ○ RSVP phone number or e-mail
- ○ RSVP deadline

Optional elements include the following:

- ○ Significance of the event (purpose, frequency, historic importance)
- ○ Dress requirements
- ○ Directions and parking instructions
- ○ Names of prominent speakers
- ○ VIP status
- ○ Complimentary ticket enclosure

Always give attendees a deadline for responding to announcements if they must confirm attendance. This will ensure that you meet your own deadlines. If you fail to conclude arrangements for airfare or hotel rooms in time, you will lose discounts offered for advance reservations.

And, unlike a reporter, you must always add the crucial additional question:

- *How much?* In other words, what is the available budget? This piece of information will affect your event design, because many ideas will not be possible to achieve with the funds available. Telling clients that what they want is impossible given their budget is not a job for the fainthearted. On the other hand, remember that anyone who chooses to plan events is both stouthearted and has nerves made of steel! Just make sure you are tactful so that the client won't run off, never to knock at your door again.

Once you have noted answers to the basic seven questions, you need more specific information. Do your clients want to have any live entertainment at the event? What kind? What type of food and beverages would they like? How elaborate must the

▲

Staying on Top of Trends

Key to your success will be staying on top of event-planning trends. Current trends include:

- ○ *Green events.* The trend is toward planning parties with an eye on protecting the environment, from biodegradable, potato-based flatware to organic menus and limousines fueled by electricity.

- ○ *Catering stations.* Many clients prefer catering stations rather than serving sit-down dinners. Businesses find that as attendees fill their plates at stations, they tend to network and make better connections than at more formal events.

- ○ *Streamlined events.* The emphasis is on doing more with less and on working smarter. Event attendees lead busy lives and, particularly when planning corporate events, you will need to keep attendees moving and keep the day concentrated.

- ○ *Heritage-related events.* Festivals of all kinds remain popular.

- ○ *Local events.* Companies are doing what they can to reduce the need for travel. Instead of one large national event, some corporations now hold several regional events.

- ○ *"Recycled" events.* There has been a recent increase in party-pooling (i.e., two or more hosts combining their resources to produce an event) and repeat parties (i.e., reusing decor for another party the following day).

Planning Trends

- ○ *Concern for charities.* Recently, organizers of social events (e.g., birthday parties) have requested guest donations to charity in lieu of gifts. Both corporations and individuals often donate leftover food to local homeless shelters and food banks.

- ○ *Accessibility for the disabled.* The Americans with Disabilities Act requires that all publicly accessible buildings accommodate disabled people, including wheelchair space, ramps, handrails, a clear line of sight between audience and sign-language interpreter, and appropriate table heights. Many planners go even beyond what is now required by law.

- ○ *Responsible drinking.* This trend has resulted in decreased amounts of alcohol at events and in the provision of designated drivers.

props or decorations be? Do they want a photographer or videographer? Will transportation be needed? Should there be valet parking?

Add these details to your notebook. Or make copies of the Event Design Worksheet, starting on page 40, and fill one out for each event.

Adequate research is important to the success of any event you plan. Yet Goldblatt finds that the research phase often does not receive enough attention. Make sure you have asked and received answers to all the above questions before you proceed to the design phase.

Bright Idea

As a first step in social event planning, consultant Patty Sachs suggests providing every potential client with a sheet that briefly details how your company works, what the general price structure is like, etc. This strategy ensures that clients are aware you'll require a deposit and that your company does not produce events for $10 per hour!

Design Time

Your creativity comes most into play in the design phase of event planning, during which you sketch out the overall feel and look of the event. This is the time to brainstorm, either by yourself or with your employees. It's also the time to pull out and look through your idea file. (You do have one, don't you? If not, read on and take notes.) Don't forget to consult your notebook for the client's answers to the questions you asked in the research phase. These responses, especially the one regarding the event budget, will help you to thoroughly check each idea for feasibility, preferably before suggesting it to the client.

Developing Design Ideas

Sachs has the following suggestions for ensuring you are never stumped for design ideas to build on. "Attend openings, promotions, shows, and other events to study the way that they are produced," she says. "Save invitations and programs. Make 'event idea' cards, and file them in a box according to category."

If you are stumped for ideas to propose to your client, consider a theme event, always popular. Themes may be inspired by a variety of factors, including time (Roaring '20s, Medieval festival, Disco Days), place (Caribbean Island, outer space), hobbies (Night at the Theater, Spa Party, Tennis mixer), or special events (Indy 500, Academy Awards, Super Bowl).

Tip...

Smart Tip

It is a good idea not to give the client more than an overall sketch of the event design until the contract is signed. Otherwise you risk giving away the results of your creative labor for next to nothing.

▲

Elements of Style

The design phase is the time to pay close attention to the style of the event. If the client wants an elegant banquet with Victorian accents, sites like a giant hayloft or a space museum aren't good bets. (Yes, we know that's an extreme example, but you get the point.) On the other hand, a boating party followed by an open-air picnic, while not the first type of event that springs to mind, might work extremely well if the site, decor, catering, and entertainment fit the style of the event. The rest of our discussion of the design phase will focus on the four aspects of the event style, including site selection, décor, catering, and entertainment.

Selecting a Site

Your choice of site will depend on several factors. Chief among these are your client, the event budget, and the purpose of the event. Corporate events, meetings, and conventions typically take place in hotels, convention centers, meeting centers, clients' facilities, or restaurants. More elaborate corporate events may take place at exotic sites, such as on cruise ships or in resorts.

Social events can be held virtually anywhere your imagination (or your client's) will go. Possible event sites include the following:

- Fresh air (garden or park, farm or ranch, forest or meadow, back yard, beach or lake-front)
- On the move (ship or yacht, train, double-decker bus, trolley)
- Home, sweet home (house, mansion, castle)
- Child's play (zoo, theme park, children's restaurant, circus, children's theater, art center)
- Cultured pearls (university, museum, planetarium, symphony hall)
- Good sports (swimming pool, miniature golf course, baseball diamond, skating rink, tennis club)

When looking at sites, remember that price is one of many factors to consider. Look at the entire package of amenities and services offered. Make sure you understand what is included in price quotes. Some sites include taxes and service charges in their quotes while others do not. Keep in mind that a site with a low-end quote may turn out to be more expensive than one with a high-end quote if the former charges for services the latter offers for free. Carefully compare services and prices. Consultant Patty Sachs offers an additional piece of advice, "Get the reactions of others who have rented the site for events."

Beware!

Many sites have restrictions. Historic sites, for instance, may have limits on the types of décor. Other sites may not allow alcohol to be served. Don't set yourself—and your client—up for a nasty surprise. Always thoroughly check that a location offers all of the amenities your client requires. Remember, too, that if the site is outdoors, you'll need to make provisions for electricity, water, and restroom facilities, as well as for shelter from inclement weather.

Creating the Perfect Decor

Creativity is a key element in this aspect of event planning. For this reason, the decor margin of profit can be as much as 40 percent for a large, elaborate event. If you are handling the decor yourself, remember to allow for the creative work involved. Do not give clients estimates until you are sure of what they want and how much time and effort you will spend to achieve it.

Perhaps your strength as a planner is in your ability to handle the myriad details involved in organizing the event, but you feel less confident in your ability to design décor. Then, don't be afraid to ask others for help. Work with florists and caterers who can not only help you design décor for specific events but also help you to build your own design sense.

Décor elements can include, but are not limited to, the following:

- Constructed set elements (castle, bridge, storefront)
- Painted backdrops (mural, play scenery)
- Props (fountain, trellis, palm trees, furniture)
- Fabric displays (swags, drapings)
- Floral treatments (centerpieces, greenery drapes, garlands, bouquets)
- Lighting elements (spotlight, strobes, small white lights)
- Historical elements (period pieces, documents)
- Signage (banner, signposts)
- Guests themselves (period costumes, wearing fluorescent lights)
- Accessories (candles, balloons)

Depending on the size of the event, your own background, and how important each element of the decor is judged to be, you may have separate vendors for each element or you may do it all yourself.

Smart Tip

Tip...

Many continuing adult education programs offer inexpensive courses in flower arranging, centerpiece creation, and decorating. Consider taking some of these courses to boost your creative inspiration!

Simply Beautiful

Liese Gardner and Susan Terpening, authors of *The Art of Event Design* (Premedia Business Magazines & Media Inc.), provide the following decor tips:

○ To make a bold statement, consider a black-and-white color scheme, adding a fashionable accent color for flair.

○ Scale is very important. If possible, use huge decor elements at entranceways to create an impact and a sense of enormous space.

○ Skillful repetition is also key to successful design. But use your instincts, and avoid repeating your main elements too many times.

○ Streamline your event decor by looking at all elements of the design and taking away anything that's not absolutely necessary. Remember, less is more!

If you are doing the decor yourself, remember to pay extra attention to the entrance and reception areas. These are the areas that make the first impression and where the majority of photographs will be taken. Also keep in mind that lighting is often a neglected decor element but is extremely important to mood and ambiance. In fact, event planning veteran Martin Van Keken says, "It's the single most important element of an event." Lighting is also useful for creating special effects and for enhancing themes.

The goal of the event and the age of its attendees both help determine the use of space, in terms of decor and seating arrangements. For example, if the main purpose is to provide networking opportunities, then guests need to be able to move around freely, and the event site should be relatively free of chairs and other potential obstacles. On the other hand, if the attendees are all senior citizens, extra seating will be needed to ensure comfort.

Food, Glorious Food

Food and beverages have a well-established role in successful events. Earlier, we noted a trend involving increased attention to the nutritional value of foods. In addition, food presentation (i.e., the way food looks in a display or on a plate) is receiving a lot of attention. The French have said it for centuries: "C'est la presentation

Tip...

Smart Tip
Fountains remain popular design elements, including chocolate fondue fountains and trendy fountains serving Cosmopolitans.

Thinking Outside the Box . . . or Basket!

When a seasonal club approached Lauren Polastri to plan their summer events, she had to think outside of the box.

I was approached by this huge yacht club with very limited kitchen and cooking facilities. They didn't want a buffet. In the past, they felt that the lines had been too long and that buffets weren't appropriate for some of their black-tie events. They also had a very set budget. So, I came up with this idea to use baskets. Each table of ten or 12 guests is presented with a beautiful basket, overflowing with food. For instance, at the 4th of July party, the basket was filled with lovely foods like filet mignon; shrimp kabobs; and potato, green bean, and pasta salads. The baskets are passed around each table. It's very social and interactive since people have to speak to one another as the basket is passed and it's an elegant way to present the food—and it means no more standing in long buffet lines! Now, I am having brides ask for the same presentation, using baskets at each table.

qui compte" (Presentation is what counts). The rest of us are only now catching on. If you are planning small events, you are less likely to encounter food sculptures or other more elaborate presentation effects, but always make sure you hire a caterer who not only pays attention to the taste and nutritional content of food, but also provides a variety of food colors and textures.

If you discuss food choices with clients, you will undoubtedly consider customer preference and budget. Also keep in mind the following aspects of the event:

- *Formality*. Simpler foods work best with relaxed occasions. Reserve fancier food items for more formal events.
- *Theme or region*. If the event has a theme, match the food to it. When appropriate, consider regional cuisine.
- *Seating plan*. Foods requiring a knife and fork are best reserved for sit-down events. If guests will be standing, such as at a cocktail party, finger foods are preferable. Finger foods should be bite-sized.
- *Overall "look" of serving stations or tables*. As noted above, food color is important to the presentation effect. A banquet choice of chicken, mashed potatoes, cauliflower, and white rolls suffers from several problems, among which is that all these items are white!

Encourage clients to choose foods with vivid colors like red, orange, and purple. (Yes, purple. And no, we are not suggesting dyed foods—purple cabbage makes a terrific garnish.)

That's Entertainment

The possibilities for entertaining guests are virtually limitless. Keep in mind that usually the more involved the guests are, the better time they'll have. Just to get you started, here are a few ideas:

- Performing arts (dancers, musicians, singers, actors, comedians)
- Mysticism (fortune tellers, palm readers, magicians)
- Circus (clowns, acrobats, jugglers, tightrope walkers)
- Interactive (caracaturist)
- Carnival (games, rides)
- Kids' fun (puppets, mimes, robots, ventriloquists, balloon artists, petting zoo)
- Pastimes and sports (croquet, horseshoes, miniature golf, volleyball)
- Period performances (jousting, chariot races, wandering minstrels)

Smart Tip

Tip...

When it comes to food, trends seem to develop more quickly than the proverbial eye blink, so it is essential that you keep your ear to the ground—or in this case, to the kitchen door—to stay on top of the foodie "in's" and "out's." For instance, remember when green tea was the hip, healthy drink? Those days are over. Hipsters are drinking yerba matte from Argentina, the "new green tea." Keep in tune by reading the food section of your local paper, by subscribing to _Gourmet, Bon Appetit, Food and Wine,_ or a food magazine of your choice, and by checking out what the hot new restaurants in your area are serving. Staying on top of culinary news will give you a competitive edge.

The Main Event

Once you have interviewed the client and done some preliminary brainstorming, you should have enough information to fill out the Event Design Worksheet," starting on page 40.

If you are just starting out in the event planning industry, make sure you have this worksheet or something similar filled out before you provide the client with a proposal containing an event cost estimate (see Chapter 8). Note that your proposal need not detail every aspect of the event design.

Be aware that the production of a proposal is time consuming and potentially expensive, especially if you include photographs or sketches. Sachs points out that

Seating Chart

The following are the typical seating configurations for different event types:

○ *Banquet rounds.* This is the most frequently used seating for social functions involving food. Round tables are 60 or 72 inches in diameter and normally seat from eight to 12 people.

○ *Reception.* Smaller round tables with cocktail and food stations throughout a room.

○ *One long oval or rectangular table.* This type of table is ideal for small parties or meetings in which close interaction is desired.

○ *U-shape, T-shape, and E-shape, hollow square, and hollow circle styles.* These configurations are all created using 8-foot-long tables. These seating plans are ideal for committee or staff meetings.

○ *Classroom-, theater-, or auditorium-style.* Rows of chairs face the front of the room, either with or without desks. This seating style is used for corporate events involving presentations.

only the larger companies producing high-end events can afford to provide clients with free proposals. You should receive a consultation fee (she suggests about $150), which can be applied toward a client's event if he or she hires you.

Maximizing the appeal of an event means making sure that all five senses are engaged. Engaged, but not overwhelmed. Goldblatt suggests providing not only sensory areas but also "neutral zones" whenever possible, especially if the event is a large one. Before finalizing the design, you should mentally "walk through" the event. What will guests see, hear, smell, taste, and touch?

Once you have a signed contract and a design that meets client approval, it is time to organize the details of the event.

Smart Tip

Tip...

Include emergency phone numbers in your event records in case problems arise. Suppliers and any vendors not on-site for the event should give you numbers to call if, for example, any equipment malfunctions. Also, store these phone numbers in your cell phone for one-touch dialing.

▲

Measuring Up

Use the following industry tips to help gauge serving requirements:

○ A gallon of liquid (punch, coffee, etc.) fills approximately 20 standard (8-oz) cups.

○ As a general rule, 30 percent of the coffee you provide should be decaffeinated and 70 percent regular, except in the evening, when the numbers are closer to 50 percent each.

○ Assuming a comfortable room temperature at the event venue, 65 percent of morning beverages should be hot and 35 percent cold. In the afternoon, beverages should be 35 percent hot and 65 percent cold. Guidelines are more difficult in the evening when the beverages offered depend greatly on the type of event.

○ Provide one server for every 20 to 25 people at a sit-down meal.

○ Provide one bartender for every 75 to 100 people, unless the event is primarily for cocktails. In that case, you may need one bartender for every 25 to 30 guests.

All Important Organization

During this decision-intensive phase, you will rent the site, hire vendors, and take care of even more details than you might believe possible. You'll be on the phone until your ear is numb. But before you do any of this, make sure you have a contact person (either the client or someone acting on the client's behalf) with whom you'll discuss all major decisions. Ideally, this person's name should appear on the client agreement (see Chapter 4). Having a designated individual helps ensure that communication lines are kept open. Also, social events in particular sometimes suffer from the "too many cooks" syndrome. Having one designated contact helps you avoid being caught in the middle of disagreements. "You don't want to find yourself caught between mother and daughter or husband and wife," says Sachs.

Generally speaking, the bigger the event, the more lead time required to plan it. Major conventions are planned years in advance.

Tip...

Smart Tip
Be sure to have a headset for both your home phone and your cell phone. Many states now require headsets for drivers using their cell phones. As an event planner, you will spend many hours on the phone, making a headset a must-have piece of equipment.

Although you may not be arranging events on such a grand scale, you do need to allow at least a few months for events like corporate picnics, reunions, or large parties.

Begin by arranging for the following:

- *Site.* If applicable, you must have a signed contract for the site before any other plans can be made. *Do not proceed with your planning until you have locked up the site location.*

- *Air travel.* If your client's event requires it, air travel arrangements should be made as soon as possible after signing the site contract. With sufficient lead time,

Beware!
Unfortunately, there are some limousine companies that have proved to be less than reliable. For instance, they might send cars with malfunctioning air conditioners on the muggiest day of the summer. Help to ensure first-rate limousine service by checking with the National Limousine Association at www.limo.org.

you can usually obtain group rates from most major airlines. Select a company that has experience with group travel and can advise you of the lowest fares available and the best routes for your attendees. Again, the sooner you purchase tickets, generally the greater the savings you'll realize for your client.

- *Ground transportation.* Depending on the event and the number of attendees, you may need to contract with a limousine service, a bus company, or a car rental agency to meet your needs. Normally, planners should arrange for attendee transportation to and from the airport, for guided tours, and to special events outside the site. Before you choose ground transportation services, compare the reservation, deposit, payment, and cancellation policies of several companies to make sure you get the best service.

- *Vendors.* Make sure you have done your homework and that you possess signed contracts.

Organization Checklist

Once these major decisions have been made, you will have many more details to deal with. On page 43, there's a checklist to help you, although you may not need to do all these things. Time frames are shown in a range to accommodate a variety of event sizes. Use this checklist and fill in any other tasks particular to your event.

Balancing the Logistics

Effective organization requires logistical ability and knowledge of the following types of information, among others:

Event Design Worksheet

1. *Who?*
   Type of guest: _____
   Age group: _____
   Number of guests: _____
   Degree of guest participation: _____

2. *What?*
   Type of event: _____
   _____
   Style: _____
   _____
   Theme? _____
   _____

3. *When?*
   Date: _____
   Start time: _____
   End time: _____
   Invitations to be sent? _____

4. *Where?*
   Site (or site type): _____
   Guest lodging to be arranged? _____
   Transport to be arranged? _____
   Security services needed? _____
   Emergency personnel needed? _____
   Special needs to be accommodated? _____

5. *Why?*
   Goal/purpose of the event: _____
   _____
   Publicity for the event? _____
   _____
   _____

6. *How?*

How should guests remember the event? (Prioritize the following.)

○ *Site*

Type of facility: _____

Location: _____

Accommodations: _____

Amenities: _____

○ *Décor*

Major elements: _____

_____

Additional elements: _____

_____

○ *Catering*

Type of cuisine: _____

Beverages/alcohol: _____

Type of service (cocktail, buffet, seated table service): _____

_____

○ *Entertainment*

Music: _____

_____

Performance: _____

_____

Activities: _____

_____

Speaker: _____

_____

7. *How Much?*

What is the budget? _____

Range of flexibility? _____

_____

_____

_____

- How many people you can comfortably get into a room. This depends on the purpose of the event, the activities involved, and the space taken up by the décor.

- Whether one buffet line will service 350 people. It won't!

- Where to put food service stations. In areas with easy access for replenishing.

- How long to allow for a cocktail reception. Allow 30 minutes to an hour.

- How to let guests know to begin eating. An invocation or some other cue should do the trick.

- How to be sure guests will have finished eating before the scheduled activities begin. Build in a little extra time.

Coordinating the Event

After you have made the initial plans, turn your attention to each of the activities that form a part of the overall event. At this point, your goal is to ensure that everyone is on the same wavelength. Good communication skills are important. Make sure all vendors have at least a general idea of the overall event schedule. Even more important, vendors should be clear about what is expected of them, and when. Vendor arrival times should appear in the contracts, but verify those times anyway. This is a "check and recheck" period. Make sure all your staff members know their roles. Remember, good communication is key. "Big projects can get out of control very quickly," cautions planner Joyce Barnes-Wolff.

Use a notebook (or your computer) to track the progress of each aspect of the event. While you will not record items that a vendor is responsible for providing (e.g., flowers ordered by the florist or food items the caterer orders), your tracking system should include all supplies and equipment your own business orders, as well as the names of suppliers, so you can verify them quickly. Use separate lists for items purchased and rented. The Organizational Checklist on page 43 is a sample of the information you might want to include in your records.

To maximize the effectiveness of your coordination efforts—not to mention minimize your headaches—remember:

- Delegate when possible.

- Anticipate change and be flexible.

> **Tip...**
>
> **Smart Tip**
> As this chapter illustrates, event planning is a virtual juggling act. You are project manager, coordinator, creative designer, and more. Because of the immense detail required to plan any event, keep careful notes. You may be tempted to forgo this process, thinking you can keep certain details stored in your mind rather than on paper. Don't be tempted. What isn't written down is likely to become lost.

Organization Checklist

Stage I (30–90 days before the event)
- ❏ Reserve venue and accommodations
- ❏ Review budget (periodically)
- ❏ Contract with vendors
- ❏ Investigate licensing requirements
- ❏ Develop a marketing plan, if needed
- ❏ Make note of can't-miss dates in vendor contracts
- ❏ Invite speakers (after confirming availability)
- ❏ Schedule entertainment
- ❏ Send announcements or invitations to attendees
- ❏ Select audiovisual materials
- ❏ Contact suppliers of any items you handle yourself (e.g., rental items)

Stage II (15–60 days before the event)
- ❏ Send second announcements with information on hotel and travel arrangements
- ❏ Complete the activities list and the menus
- ❏ Verify arrangements with client, vendors, and suppliers
- ❏ Complete contingency/emergency plans
- ❏ Prepare evaluations
- ❏ Prepare list of temporary help needed

Stage III (10–30 days before the event)
- ❏ Finalize event setups, transportation, and guest accommodations
- ❏ Confirm reservation of audiovisual equipment
- ❏ Arrange for transport of audiovisual equipment to the site
- ❏ Submit a room list and pay a deposit to the site
- ❏ Complete airline reservations
- ❏ Hire temporary help
- ❏ Conduct orientation meeting/training of temporary help
- ❏ Send any event-related tickets to attendees

Stage IV (5–10 days before the event)
- ❏ Send all printed materials to the site (keep master copies for yourself in case materials are lost)
- ❏ Contact all vendors to confirm

▲

- Have a backup plan for any critical aspects of the event.
- Share critical timing elements with vendors and site personnel.

Another way to minimize your headaches is to use a checklist like the one on page 45.

"You Cannot Rest on Your Laurels"

As all event planners will tell you, "You're only as good as your last event." Lauren Polastri, of The Other Woman, agrees. "You absolutely cannot rest on your laurels. You need to be fresh and energized for every event."

One crucial test of an event's success is customer satisfaction. The goal, of course, is to end up with a client who will sing your praises up and down the street, shouting it from rooftops. This is the client who will hire you again, perhaps for an even bigger (and more expensive) event. This is also the customer who will provide the famous word-of-mouth advertising for you.

Having a blissfully happy client does not mean you're home free, however. You can always improve, and additional evaluation will help you to do so. If you have employees, a round-table post-event discussion can bring to light aspects you may not have considered. Collect input from every team member.

Your evaluation procedure should include an actualization, i.e., an accounting of your company's investment (hours worked, costs incurred) in the event. This procedure helps verify that you are charging clients enough to make a profit.

There are several other ways to evaluate the success of an event. One is to have a trained individual observe it and give you feedback. Such an individual could be an event planning consultant. Depending on the consultant's experience level and the type of event, you can expect to pay anywhere from $25 to $50 per hour, for 10 or more hours. A shorter session would probably mean a higher hourly rate.

This individual could also be a lay person, however. If you know someone who hosts extremely successful parties, consider asking that person to observe your event. Or get someone who plans fundraising events to help you in return for a generous donation.

> ## ! Beware!
> Lauren Polastri of The Other Woman learned the hard way about confirming the delivery of rental items. "I arrived at a small event and found that the items that were to be delivered the day before had not arrived. Fortunately, I was able to send one of my employees to pick everything up and the day was saved. I learned to always check on rentals the day before. Make sure the numbers are correct and that everything is clean and in good condition. Rentals can absolutely make or break an event."

Sample Tracking Record—Items Rented

Item	Quantity	Use	Supplier	Date Received	Cost (Total)
linens-round	30	tables	AJ Linens	7/15/07	$174.80
linens-rect.	10	buffet tables	AJ Linens	7/15/07	$35.67
lanterns	25	lighting (grounds)	Lux Inc.	not received	$150.00

Coordination Checklist

Stage I (Day before the event)
- ❑ Review the program with site directors
- ❑ Troubleshoot with staff to overcome any problems
- ❑ Confirm arrival of all printed and audiovisual materials
- ❑ Confirm delivery of all rental items (or else pick them up)
- ❑ Tour the facility to confirm setups
- ❑ Ensure that all vendors' contact numbers are stored in your cell phone

Stage II (Day of the event)
- ❑ Check signage
- ❑ Verify that all rental items have arrived—tick them off
- ❑ Inspect all setups at least one hour before the event begins, checking off items in your notebook
- ❑ Test all microphones and audiovisual equipment
- ❑ Distribute evaluations at the event

Stage III (After the event)
- ❑ Return any kegs and recover deposits
- ❑ Distribute tips
- ❑ Write thank-you letters to client, site personnel, and vendors
- ❑ Review and approve all vendor bills for payment
- ❑ Have post-event evaluation meeting (it is important to have this meeting while the event is still fresh in everyone's mind)
- ❑ Compile all event data in one file and store in records

▲

Sample Survey

Please rate the following aspects of this event by circling your response:

1. *Décor*	Excellent	Good	Average	Fair	Poor
2. *Food/beverage*	Excellent	Good	Average	Fair	Poor
3. *Entertainment*	Excellent	Good	Average	Fair	Poor
4. *Service*	Excellent	Good	Average	Fair	Poor
5. *Friendliness of personnel*	Excellent	Good	Average	Fair	Poor
6. *Service*	Excellent	Good	Average	Fair	Poor

We appreciate any comments you can provide:

_____

_____

_____

Thank you for your help!

Another way to evaluate an event is to get feedback from other industry professionals working at the event. The caterer and the bartender, among others, might be able to provide you with suggestions.

If the event is open to the general public (e.g., a community event), consider surveying the guests at the event. You can get immediate feedback this way, and most people you approach will cooperate. Talk to as many people as time allows, and take notes. Remember, the feedback you receive may not be very balanced. People may be swept up in the mood of the moment. Without time for them to step back and reflect, they may provide unwarrantedly positive or negative feedback. Conducting a mail or phone survey can eliminate this disadvantage, but you will not get the same level of cooperation. A response rate of 10 percent is considered average, so you will need to survey many more guests than you would with a face-to-face survey.

However you conduct your survey, keep your questions to a minimum and keep them short. You can have people fill out the sample survey above at the event, or you could mail it to attendees.

Whatever combination of strategies you choose, Goldblatt advises, don't wait until the end of the event before collecting at least some feedback. Unless you know about them in time, it's impossible to correct details that might make the difference between an average event and a stand-out one. He also cautions that evaluation is another phase that receives too little attention.

Finally, carefully consider the evaluation. Don't simply tuck the responses in your desk drawer. Some of the evaluations may sting a bit if they are critical but view these criticisms as constructive and make plans to address these issues at your next event. This attention to detail could enable you to take your events from so-so to smashing successes.

Now that you know what is involved in each stage of the event planning process, we turn our attention to what you need to do to get your own business up and running. So grab a strong cup of coffee, or a large chocolate bar, or both. Then read on as we tackle the necessary paperwork.

4

Getting Started

This chapter details much of what you will need to do before you open your doors. We will cover naming your business, determining its business structure, and finding a location. We will also take a brief pass at acquiring the necessary licenses, permits, and business insurance. (Well, you didn't expect every aspect to be fascinating, did you?) Finally, we will provide some sample documents you'll need to run your business.

It's All in a Name

There is no question that the right name can draw your target market to you. It can also single out your event planning business from others and keep it sharp in clients' memories. Before you decide on a name, consider what kind of planning you want to do, the scope you want your business to have, and whether you want to convey a particular image. Will you have a highly specialized service (e.g., only birthday parties) or an extremely general one (e.g., social and corporate events of all kinds)? Will your service be local, national, or international? Do you want to produce only high-budget events, or will you work in any price range? Depending on your answers to these questions, a good name for your business could consist of any of the following:

- *Description of your service* (e.g., Event Planning Inc.)

  Advantages: Helps potential clients hone in on you.

  Disadvantages: Creativity sometimes suffers.

- *The type of event you specialize in* (e.g., Birthday Bashes)

  Advantages: Helps clients find you. You'll get fewer calls for types of events that you don't plan.

  Disadvantages: Your specialization might change. What if you decide to do anniversary parties, too?

- *Your name* (e.g., Ann Smith Inc.)

  Advantages: People you meet while networking need remember only your name. If you use your full name, you may improve your personal credit rating as you build your business.

  Disadvantages: Customers won't know what type of business this is. Worse, the IRS could confuse you and your company. And if your company goes under, your personal credit rating may suffer.

Finally, if you choose to sell your business at some point, your name will become a liability. Prospective buyers prefer to buy a company that is not associated with a specific name. If Jane Doe were to buy this company and then change the name to Jane Doe, Inc., she would lose the name recognition that Ann Smith worked to build. Although you may not envision selling your company, you may at some point consider a career change and choose to sell your event planning business.

- *Qualities your business embodies* (e.g., Elegant Evenings)

   Advantages: Helps establish the image you want to create.

   Disadvantages: Vagueness may make it tough for clients to find you. Also, this kind of name pigeonholes your business. You'll probably not be hired to produce a reunion or picnic.

- *Indications of the scope of your business* (e.g., Bloomington Event Planners Ltd.)

   Advantages: Anyone looking under city listings will find you.

   Disadvantages: Your scope might change. What if you want to branch out to other cities?

- *A combination of the above* (e.g., Benden's Classic Parties)

   Advantages and disadvantages: The whole is not necessarily the sum of the parts. Consider carefully the advantages and disadvantages of each part of a combination name to see which apply.

The outline above is not an exhaustive one, but it contains some of the best ideas for creating a name that will make your business a standout in event planning. Industry expert and consultant Patty Sachs cautions against limiting yourself by choosing too specific a name. Words like perfect, elegant, and exquisite lock you into formal or high-priced events, she says. Exciting words like fabulous, fantastic, and incredible are reserved for theme parties and entertaining events. On the other hand, if you're going to be highly specialized, she suggests names like Open House Planning, His 'N' Hers Parties, Wedding Weekends, and so on. Also, she cautions, "The word 'affair' has been done to death."

Lauren Polastri, of The Other Woman event planning, took her name from a customer. Before she officially launched her business, she did some event planning for a friend and neighbor. He started referring to her as "the other woman," and the name stuck. Polastri says her dad warned her that the name might by off-putting to some clients but she has

> **Bright Idea**
>
> Stop periodically and write out two lists: a "Priorities in my business life" list and an "Actual time spent" list. Compare the lists. Are you spending the greater proportion of your working life on the activities to which you give a high ranking? If not, maybe it's time to reorganize.

▲

found that customers like the good humor of this name and that the name reflects the good nature and energy she brings to her successful business.

Many event planners select a name that will put them at the top of an alphabetical listing, for instance in the telephone directory. Check your local listings to see if this works for your business. AAA Event Planning may position your listing in first place but the name is not very informative. Don't sacrifice content for this prime position.

If you buy an existing business, you can take an element from the business's former name, or even use the whole name. New York City planner Jaclyn Bernstein, DMCP, kept half of the former name when she took over an event planning business. Thus her company's name had both a familiar ring for clients and enough of a difference to remind them that ownership had changed.

The Name Game

After you've short-listed some ideas, ask yourself the following questions about each name:

○ *Is it easy to pronounce?* People are reluctant to say a name they're unsure of its pronunciation. This reluctance could be fatal in an industry that relies heavily on word-of-mouth advertising.

○ *Is it short enough?* Length affects ease of pronunciation. Plus, you and your employees will have to say this name all day on the phone and still have time to do other tasks. Thus Supercallifragilistickexpial delicious Inc. is probably not the best choice, even if you specialize in children's events. (This name suffers from other problems, too, but we won't go into those.)

○ *Is it easy and logical to spell?* If somebody hears your company name but can't find it in the phone book because of a spelling problem, you will lose potential clients. For this reason—and others—don't opt for a silly spelling of a common word. For instance, don't even think of a name like Kountry Kids Parties. Clients looking under "c" for country will be frustrated and unlikely to find your listing.

○ *Is it memorable?* If possible, avoid a name that sounds too ordinary. Steer clear of hyperbole, though. Names should be meaningful and substantive.

When you have selected a name, take the time to make sure the name is not trademarked by another company. Even if you plan to keep your event planning business small, it is a good idea to check for trademarks. You can do this for free at www.uspto.gov. Also, check popular search engines like Google and Yahoo! to see if the name you have chosen is already used for another web site.

Registering Your Company Name

Most states mandate that you register your fictitious company name officially to ensure that it is unique. This is generally done through the county and is known as filing a DBA ("doing business as") statement. If the name you chose is already being used, you will be asked to choose something else. For this reason, it's a good idea to have a backup name or two. There is a nominal ($30–$60) cost for this service.

A good name is well worth the effort you'll put into finding it. With some thought, you can end up with a name as unique as your business.

Choosing a Business Location

The type of events you'll plan and the size of your business are among the factors that will determine where you set up shop. Event planning businesses can be run from home, in retail or commercial space, or from a vehicle.

If you're starting small, a homebased event planning business may be the ideal choice for you. This option keeps overhead low and saves travel time to and from the office. One potential problem is that friends and family might drop in at all hours because you're "not really working." Be firm. Set up business hours and stick to them.

You may find that you need more space than your home office can provide. In this case, retail or commercial space can be the perfect setup for you, especially if you expect to have some foot traffic or if you specialize in a particular type of event. Deborah Williams and Kim Quigley, who plan both corporate and social events, decided to locate their business in the now-trendy

Tip...

Smart Tip
Whatever your location, consider the following points:

○ Planners of local parties do well in central locations.

○ Convention planners should locate near the major convention sites and hotels in their cities; similarly, a meeting planner should be situated in a central business district.

○ If you plan nonlocal events, your proximity to an airport may be paramount.

Deep Ellum, a historical, artsy area of Dallas. Jaclyn Bernstein maintains her business in a fast-paced business district in midtown Manhattan. This location is important for her company because she focuses on corporate events.

The disadvantage of renting space is primarily the cost. Rent, utilities, phone lines, and parking are all considerable expenses. Downtown locations are especially costly.

Commercial leases are often more complicated than residential leases. Before signing, check with an attorney. Commercial leases are difficult to break so proceed with caution.

Executive suites also make sense for event planning businesses. They provide you with a good business address, a professional atmosphere, phones, and other business equipment. Sometimes executive suites will even provide a shared secretary.

If you go to clients rather than having them come to you, a car or van might work as your headquarters. Keep in mind, however, that you'll have to either invest in a laptop computer or keep part of your office elsewhere.

Wherever you locate, make sure that your business does not violate zoning ordinances, rental agreements, and the community welfare. This holds true for all kinds of event planners.

Consider stockpiling space if you expect to grow quickly or store a lot of equipment so you won't have to move.

> ### Smart Tip ... Tip...
> If you opt for a home-based business, you must allocate a space that is to be used solely for your business. It could be a small area, a desk tucked into the corner of the dining room, for instance, but it must be devoted to your event planning business. It is also wise to have a separate phone line for your business. Nothing will kill your credibility faster than using your home phone line with its answering machine featuring your three-year-old singing the theme song from "Dora, The Explorer." This is not professional. Have a separate line and a separate answering machine. This will help when tax times rolls around since your business phone expenses will be deductible. And, while on the subject of phone etiquette, never put a client on hold to speak with another client. Let your answering machine pick up any incoming calls you can't answer yourself.

Selecting a Business Structure

You have to do more legal stuff for your newborn business than new parents have to worry about. On the other hand, you'll probably be way ahead in the sleep department, which means you'll have some working brain cells available for the tasks that lie ahead of you.

Types of Business Forms

Congratulations! You have named your business, have your DBA in hand, and you are considered the owner of a legitimate business. Now, you will need to make the decision to operate as one of four business entities: a sole proprietorship, a corporation, a partnership, or a limited liability company (LLC).

Sole Proprietors

Many event planners choose to operate as sole proprietors because it's the easiest type of business to form. All you have to do is file a DBA, as discussed above, then open a business checking account in that name. You can use your personal credit card to pay for business expenditures, yet you still get tax benefits like business expense deductions. But there is a downside to the sole proprietorship. You are personally liable for any losses, bankruptcy claims, legal actions, and so on. That can wipe out both your personal and business assets if major problems arise.

Industry expert Patty Sachs operated her own business in Minneapolis as a sole proprietorship for many years and never had a problem with this legal form.

Joyce Barnes-Wolff, who runs her own event planning business in Ohio, also has a sole proprietorship. "It's easy and quick," she says. "For me, this works the best." However, most banks are not eager to lend money to sole proprietorships, she points out.

General Partnership

Perhaps you are planning to work with another event planner as you form your business. Then you are forming a general partnership. Partnerships are easier to form than corporations, and you don't have to file any documents to make them legal. Each partner is responsible for the actions of the other so it's a good idea to have a partnership agreement that is crystal clear regarding what each partner is responsible for.

Limited Liability Company

A third type of business entity is the limited liability company, or LLC, which combines the tax structure of a partnership, yet protects the business owner from personal liability. This structure protects each partner's personal interests.

Corporations

The last type of business arrangement is the corporation. It is established as a totally separate legal entity from the business owner. Establishing a corporation requires filing articles of incorporation, electing officers, and holding an annual meeting. Not many event planners choose this route initially because the costs are prohibitive, and the company must pay corporate taxes. On the other hand, a corporation will find it easier to obtain financing, which would be useful if you decided to franchise your business or expand in a big way.

Although the process for creating a corporate structure is more complicated and expensive than creating other structures, it does offer protection to event planners and their assets. A corporate structure is often advantageous to a business because the corporation exists as a separate entity. It alone is legally responsible for its actions and debts. As an employee of the corporation, your personal assets are protected in most situations, even though you may own all or most of the stock. Deborah Williams and Kim Quigley turned their partnership into a C corporation on the advice of their attorney. "You could lose your home, your car, everything, with a partnership," says Deborah.

> **Bright Idea**
> Consider sharing space with a related business. For example, you could set up shop with a party supply store or a caterer. You might not only save money but also gain referrals. If you elect to share space, however, make sure you have a clear contract stating how space and responsibilities will be shared. Also, be sure to share space with a well-respected party. Sharing space with a less then reliable caterer will not boost your business!

According to industry expert John Daly, the decision to incorporate depends partly on how much you have at stake. In his opinion, small events are not usually a problem, but once you're doing huge ceiling treatments, you don't want to risk wiping out your personal assets. The main points to remember? Incorporation protects you. However, increased paperwork and taxes are disadvantages.

If deciding on a legal form for your business keeps you up at night, consider two things: First, your nails will grow back. Second, as the above examples illustrate, your business structure is not carved in stone. It can be changed.

Licenses and Permits

Most cities and counties require business operators to obtain various licenses and permits to comply with local regulations. For everyday operation of an event planning business, you may need the following:

- *Business license*: ensures proper zoning and parking
- *Vendor's permit* (varies from state to state): allows you to buy and resell
- *Health department permit*: if you also cater events and thus handle food

The Right Idea

Any original idea in a unique form can be protected under U.S. copyright. This includes cartoon characters, sculptures, paintings, plays, maps, songs, scripts, photos, books, and poems, to name but a few. There are five classes of copyrights:

1. *Class TX*: Nondramatic literary works (fiction, nonfiction, advertising copy, textbooks, etc.)
2. *Class PA*: Works of the performing arts (drama, music, choreography, etc.)
3. *Class SR*: Sound recordings (independent of musical or literary works)
4. *Class VA*: Works of the visual arts (pictures, graphics, models, maps, ads, etc.)
5. *Class RE*: Renewal registration (works originally copyrighted before January 1, 1978—all classes)

Why, you may ask, do you need to know about this? If you come up with an original logo for your service or for a type of event that you produce, you might want to copyright that logo. Similarly, you might write a script for a particular type of original event (e.g., a murder mystery/dessert party) and want to copyright it.

To apply for a copyright, send a copy of the work with an official form and a $30 application fee to the Copyright Office, Library of Congress, 101 Independence Ave. SE, Washington, DC 20559, (202) 707-3000. For more information, consult its web site at www.copyright.gov.

- *Liquor, wine, and beer licenses*: if you yourself serve alcohol
- *Sign permit*: covers size, location, and sometimes the type of sign you may use
- *County permits*: may be applicable if you are located outside city limits

Depending on the event, you may also need the following:

- *Fire marshall permit*: for large gatherings, events with fireworks, or the display of a vehicle indoors
- *Special event permit*: if you'll be using city property
- *Street closure permit*: for closing off a street (e.g., a block party or arts festival)
- *Parade permit*: self-explanatory!

Check local regulations to see which of the above licenses and permits you'll need. But no matter where your event will take place, you may need to apply for the following types of permission:

- *Copyright permission.* The two major U.S. music-licensing companies, Broadcast Music International (BMI) and the American Society of Composers, Authors, and Publishers (ASCAP), enforce their rights to collect fees. You may need copyright permission to use text materials, music, audiovisual displays, photographs, drawings, ads, drama pieces, or any number of a variety of materials. Always check for the copyright of any materials you use in an event. We do not suggest this lightly or out of a desire to "cover our act," as it were. The fact is, many artists and companies take copyright infringement very seriously. Therefore, so should you.

- *Trademark permission.* Be aware that distinctive trademarks are protected. Trademarks apply to products. For example, you may need permission to use any relevant brand names on literature you circulate about an event or about your business.

Even if your event planning business does not need a particular type of permit, always make sure that your vendors are properly licensed and have the appropriate permits.

Choosing Insurance

Knowing what kind of insurance to carry and how much to obtain is an important aspect of good risk management. Don't view insurance as an option. It is absolutely imperative that you have insurance before you plan any event.

As the owner of an event planning business, you are most likely to need the following types of insurance:

- *General liability insurance.* This is the one type of insurance you must carry, and every business owner interviewed for this book had it. Many event sites will be unavailable to you if you don't carry this coverage. General liability insurance protects a business against accidents and injuries that might occur at the event site or at your office. You may be liable for bodily injuries to customers, guests, delivery people, and other outsiders—even in cases in which you have exercised "reasonable care." As David Granger points out, "If I put down lighting and someone trips over a cord that wasn't taped down, or if one of my centerpieces catches fire, or if a stage prop falls, I need to be covered." It's a good idea to carry 1 million dollars worth of liability insurance. In fact, Dallas planner Deborah Williams says local hotels won't do business with event planners who don't carry at least 1 million dollars in liability insurance.

Beware!
If you operate your event planning business from your home, you may need additional coverage. Your homeowner's policy may be sufficient, but if you plan to store or use expensive machinery, such as a computer, or if customers or clients will visit your home for business purposes, you may want to purchase additional coverage. Set up an appointment with your agent to go over your insurance coverage.

- *Workers' compensation insurance.* If you have employees, you may also want this type of insurance. Williams has it for employees at Designs Behind the Scenes. You are liable for injury to employees at work caused by problems with equipment or working conditions. In every state, an employer must insure against potential workers' comp claims. However, employee coverage and the extent of the employer's liability vary among states.

- *Auto insurance.* Cars and trucks are sources of liability. Even if you own none, you can be liable for injuries and property damage caused by employees operating their own or someone else's car while on company business.

- *Bonding.* If you sell large numbers of airline or entertainment tickets or any of several other types of goods, you may need to carry bonding. This procedure requires you to put aside money into a separate account for reimbursing clients for tickets they purchased from you in the event your business goes under. You may also need bonding to protect you if one of your employees steals or damages something at an event site. Vendors should carry their own protection. Check your state's legal requirements.

Creating Effective Proposals and Agreements

To do business (and protect your company as you do it), you'll need a variety of documents. Invoices and purchase orders for an event planning business are, for the most part, the same as those for any other business. So we will concentrate our attention on proposals and several different kinds of agreements.

Proposals

Quite simply, proposals tell clients what you will do for them and at what cost. A proposal hits the high points of your creative idea(s) for the event. It is an important selling tool and might consist of any or all of the following elements:

- *History of your company.* Provide one if relevant.
- *Letters of reference.* Kudos from clients for whom you planned similar events work wonders.
- *Write-ups.* Often a complimentary newspaper or magazine article featuring your business is a valuable tool for selling your services to others. You may also want to include photographs.
- *Description of the event.* This is where you sell your ideas. Walk the client through the event, describing what guests see, hear, smell, taste, and touch. What emotions will guests feel?
- *Description of services.* This tells which vendors you'll hire and sketches out how you'll achieve what you write about in the description of the event.
- *Listing of additional services.* If you also will provide catering, floral design, or some other service, describe those services completely.
- *Production schedule.* This item lets the client know any pertinent details about the timing of the event, especially if there are critical aspects to arrange. If you're hosting a smaller event, you usually do not need this part of the proposal.
- *Event cost estimate.* This accompanies any proposal.

Make sure you include in your proposal an expiration date for the event cost estimate. You don't want to be expected to produce that event for the listed price five years from now!

Customers must be able to visualize the event when they read your proposal. As David Granger puts it: "Proposals need to

> **Tip...**
>
> ## Smart Tip
> We've all heard it: a picture is worth a thousand words—or more! Photos in your proposal packet can make a powerful impact on prospective clients. Good photos can help to evoke a mood and a flavor, evocations that are more difficult to capture in print. Conversely, poor quality photos could kill a deal. Consider hiring a professional photographer to capture some stellar images for you or invest in a high-quality digital camera. Check Consumer Reports (www.consumer reports.org) or ask at your local camera or discount store, for advice on buying a camera. This is money well spent.

be flowery." His colleague, Deborah Williams, agrees: "Dave is phenomenal at proposals," she adds. "When you read one of his proposals, you can just see the whole thing."

You have to figure out a way to make clients visualize the event as you have designed it, and they have to understand the quality of your work. Consider including in your proposal some photos of a previous event you planned that was similar to what the client wants. Any photos included should, of course, be vivid and lively. Jaclyn Bernstein stresses the importance of asking clients a lot of questions and listening well. Catching (and using in your proposal) exact words customers have used in discussion with you helps to convey a sense of excitement about the event, she says. Enthusiasm is important, as long as your language isn't too extreme.

Agreements

The possession of signed documents detailing all aspects of the events you produce is not only helpful but also imperative to the legal health of your business.

These are descriptions of the different types of event planning agreements.

- *Client agreements.* Once the client has agreed to hire your company, you need an official contract. The exact form this contract appears in will vary by state because you must conform to state code. If you draft your own client agreement, get a local attorney to take a look at it.

  We provide a sample agreement, starting on page 63, to give you an idea of elements you may want to include in your own agreement.

- *Vendor agreements.* Any vendor providing a service for your client's event should sign a formal agreement with your planning company. As with any legal document, get your local attorney's advice. Starting on page 65 is a sample agreement with a catering company.

  Make sure that any vendors you hire are properly insured and/or bonded. They must carry insurance to protect their companies (and you) from their negligence, bankruptcy, or lack of appearance at an event. Any forms of insurance or bonding that they carry should be listed in the vendor agreement (see page 65).

- *Site agreements.* Once you have selected the site that will best suit your client's

Beware!

Any site contract with a hotel or other lodging facility should state that if fewer rooms are occupied than expected, you will not be held responsible. Instead, attendees should be given a deadline before which they can claim a room in the reserved block at the group rate. After the deadline, any unreserved rooms are made available to the general public.

Foundation Essentials

Complete these items as you get your business started:

○ Develop and write a business plan

○ Create a powerful mission statement

○ Select a name for your company and apply for a DBA

○ Choose the best business structure for your company

○ Check local zoning laws to ensure that you are in compliance

○ Apply for the licenses and permits you will need

needs, confirm your arrangements with the site's sales representative and ask for a written contract or letter of agreement. Review the contract carefully and clarify any misunderstandings or ambiguities with the site representative. The contract should include the arrangements for guest rooms and any activities scheduled to take place at the site. Contracts should also include the site's cancellation and deposit policies.

Now that you have begun building a strong foundation for your business, in Chapter 5 we will move on to financing your business.

Sample Client Agreement

This agreement is between Right Touch Event Planning Inc. (hereafter referred to as PLANNER) and Mr. John Doe (hereafter referred to as CLIENT).

I. *PLANNER agrees to provide:*
- ○ Research, design, organization, coordination, and evaluation of the CLIENT's Silver Wedding Anniversary
- ○ A social event to begin at 8:00 P.M. on Saturday, May 23, 200x, at the CLIENT's residence and to end by 2:00 A.M. the following day
- ○ Comprehensive general liability insurance to cover damage caused by any action, or inaction, of the PLANNER or of any individuals contracted by the PLANNER
- ○ Vendors as agreed upon with the CLIENT (see attachment)
- ○ Additional staffing for the event

II. *CLIENT agrees to provide:*
- ○ The CLIENT's residence as site for the event
- ○ The CLIENT's kitchen and equipment therein for use by the caterers and bar staff
- ○ One individual to serve as decision maker for the PLANNER
- ○ Decisions in a timely manner
- ○ Homeowners' insurance to cover damage caused by an act of God or by any action, or inaction, of the CLIENT or of the CLIENT's guests

III. *FEES*

The PLANNER will receive a commission amounting to 15 percent of the total event cost. The total event cost is not to exceed $10,000.

IV. *TERMS*

The CLIENT agrees to provide payment for the services described. This payment shall be remitted to the PLANNER according to the following schedule:

Upon signing of this document:
- ○ 50 percent of total event cost, based on estimate
- ○ 25 percent of commission, based on estimated event cost

May 24, 200x:
- ○ Remainder of final event cost
- ○ Remainder of commission, based on final event cost

Sample Client Agreement, continued

V. *CANCELLATION*

Should the PLANNER cancel his or her services for any reason other than acts of God, the CLIENT shall receive a refund of all pre-paid fees, less any expenses incurred on behalf of the event. Should the CLIENT cancel the event, the following payments shall be due:

○ Cancellation more than 60 days before event: 25 percent of estimated event cost and 50 percent of commission

○ Cancellation between 15 and 60 days (incl.) before event: 75 percent of estimated event cost and 50 percent of commission

○ Cancellation less than 15 days before event: 100 percent of estimated event cost and 75 percent of commission

VI. *FORCE MAJEURE*

This agreement is automatically canceled if the event is interrupted by an act of God, by war, or by strikes.

VII. *HOLD HARMLESS and INDEMNIFICATION*

The PLANNER and CLIENT agree to hold one another harmless from negligence and to mutually indemnify.

VIII. *ACCEPTANCE OF FULL AGREEMENT*

This agreement, plus attachments, constitutes the full agreement. Any changes to this agreement must be approved in writing by both PLANNER and CLIENT. Those parties affixing signatures below agree to accept the terms and conditions of this agreement.

_____   _____

Client   *Date*

_____   _____

Planner   *Date*

Sample Vendor Agreement

This agreement is between Right Touch Event Planning Inc. (hereafter referred to as PLANNER) and Sweetness and Light Catering Inc. (hereafter referred to as VENDOR).

> EVENT DATE: May 23, 200x
> EVENT ARRIVAL TIME: 7:00 P.M.
> EVENT START TIME: 8:00 P.M.
> EVENT STOP TIME: 2:00 A.M. May 24

I. *VENDOR agrees to provide:*
- ◯ Ten trays of hors d'oeuvres, as detailed in attachment
- ◯ Buffet dinner for 40 persons, as detailed in attachment
- ◯ Dessert buffet, as detailed in attachment
- ◯ All serving equipment, including, but not limited to: trays, tongs, chafing dishes, and buffet ranges
- ◯ Serving staff, as detailed in attachment
- ◯ Cleanup crew, as detailed in attachment
- ◯ Proof of insurance

II. *PLANNER agrees to provide:*
- ◯ Complimentary parking for VENDOR and staff
- ◯ Utilities (gas, electricity, water)
- ◯ Kitchen facilities
- ◯ Tables and table linens
- ◯ One individual on-site to act as liaison with vendor
- ◯ Liability insurance for the event

III. *FEES*

PLANNER shall provide the following payment to VENDOR:

Hor d'oeuvres	$300
Buffet dinner (40 persons)	$600
Dessert buffet	$450
Serving and cleanup	$180
Subtotal:	$1,530
Less referral fee	−$80
Total:	*$1,450*

▲

Sample Vendor Agreement, continued

IV. *TERMS*

PLANNER shall pay VENDOR a deposit of 50 percent ($725) upon execution of agreement. Balance due by June 23, 200x.

V. *CANCELLATION*

If the VENDOR cancels for any reason, he or she shall forfeit all funds received or due and shall repay PLANNER any funds advanced for this event. If the PLANNER cancels for any reason, he or she must provide the following payments to VENDOR:

○ Cancellation more than 60 days before event: Refund of referral fee ($80)
○ Cancellation between 15 and 60 days (incl.) before event: 25 percent of total fee
○ Cancellation less than 15 days before event: 75 percent of total fee

VI. *FORCE MAJEURE*

This agreement is automatically canceled if the event is interrupted by an act of God, by war, or by strikes.

VII. *HOLD HARMLESS and INDEMNIFICATION*

The PLANNER and CLIENT agree to hold one another harmless from negligence and to mutually indemnify.

VIII. *ACCEPTANCE OF FULL AGREEMENT*

This agreement, plus attachments, constitutes the full agreement. Any changes to this agreement must be approved in writing by both PLANNER and CLIENT. Those parties affixing signatures below agree to accept the terms and conditions of this agreement.

_____   _____
Client   *Date*

_____   _____
Planner   *Date*

Financing Your
Business

The axiom tells us that we have to spend money to make money and, of course, this holds true in developing an event planning business. The good news, though, is that you can launch a successful business with a shoestring budget. Perhaps, you envision planning five events during your first year in business and using space in your home as your

Event Planning News

According to a recent *New York Times'* article, birthday parties for one-year-olds, particularly in urban areas, are becoming more and more elaborate. Total tabs of $100,000 are becoming, if not common, not unusual, either. Baby boomers are also celebrating their own birthdays with ever grander parties, creating many opportunities for event planners developing businesses focusing on social events.

work site. This business model is relatively inexpensive to create and highly viable. Conversely, if you are planning to launch a full-time event planning business, then the start-up costs will be considerably higher. This flexibility—part-time vs. full-time—makes event planning a terrific career opportunity for many types, from stay-at-home moms hoping to earn a few thousand dollars per year to new college graduate planning to create full-scale businesses generating full-time pay and benefits.

The First Step

Remember, first things first. Start by estimating your business expenditures over the start-up period and over the first six months of operation (see Business Expenses Worksheet on page 70). Take your figures from "My Own" column in the Start-Up Expenses Worksheet on page 20 in Chapter 2 and put these figures in the "Start-Up" column. If you have not yet made those estimates, now is the time to do so.

First, work horizontally. Add the "Start-Up" figures and the "First Six Months" figures to produce the "Total Cost" figures for each row. Then, working vertically, add up the "Total Cost" figures. The "Total Required" figure is the approximate amount you will need to start the business and keep it running for six months.

Note that this business expense worksheet includes no costs for planning particular events. You will incur these costs even if you plan no events at all. In that sense, then, these are all fixed costs. When you contract to plan an event, you should receive a deposit from each client to cover some of the immediate costs associated with producing that event (e.g., vendor deposits). The price you charge a client for planning an event will cover not only your costs for that event but also some fraction of your fixed costs.

In Chapter 8, which deals with financial management, we'll discuss how to price your planning services and how to figure out a break-even

Beware!

Do not underestimate your communications budget. If you have multiple phone lines, a cellular phone, a pager, internet access, etc., these are ongoing expenses. Joyce Barnes-Wolf estimates her monthly communications costs to be her second largest expense, after labor.

point for your business. For now, you need an approximate idea of how much money you'll require for your business and your own living expenses until your company makes a profit. Again, this is a highly personal point. Perhaps you are recently retired and want to launch a small-scale business. In other words, this will not be a primary income source. For others, their event planning businesses will be their primary income source. Making this determination greatly affects start-up costs. The recent retiree will spend substantially less on start-up costs than the person envisioning event planning as a full-time occupation.

Each company's break-even point will be different. Connecticut planner Lauren Polastri's company, The Other Woman, was profitable within the first year, in part to low start-up costs. New York City planner Jaclyn Bernstein bought an existing business, and her company was profitable within six months. Event planner Joyce Barnes-Wolff made a small profit in her business's first year. It was enough to pay herself a salary but not enough to reinvest in the company.

Once you have an idea of your capital requirements, it is time to think about your financing options.

Finding Financing

To find your best source of financing, look in the mirror. Most entrepreneurs invest their own resources first, and so should you. Your own capital is immediately available, carries no interest obligation, and requires no surrender of business equity. Event planner Martin Van Keken used money from the sale of another business. Nearly all entrepreneurs we interviewed used at least some of their own money.

If you do not have the cash reserves to launch your business, consider these sources:

- *Friends and relatives.* If you opt to turn to friends and relatives, do so with extreme care. You don't want to sour a life-long relationship by creating a financial misunderstanding with a close friend or family member. If you choose to make a financial arrangement with a friend or relative, then absolutely enlist the help of an attorney to create a contract, stipulating your obligations as well as your understanding of the transaction. Is the money a loan or a gift? Will the lender receive a percentage of the profits? Make sure that all parties understand the transaction.

> **Smart Tip**
>
> *Tip...*
>
> If you choose to finance your business using credit cards, call around for the best rates. Often, if you call and speak to a representative from your credit card company, you can negotiate a better rate than the one advertised.

Business Expenses Worksheet

	Start-Up	First Six Months	Total Cost
Rent/deposit			
Equipment			
Inventory			
Licenses and taxes			
Phone/utilities			
Payroll			
Advertising/promotion			
Legal fees and accounting			
Vehicle maintenance/mileage			
Misc. (postage, signage, office supplies, etc.)			
Total required			

- *Credit cards.* Again, proceed with extreme caution if you opt to use credit cards to finance your new business. Interest on credit cards can be crippling and could easily erase any profits you might make.

- *Equity.* Some business owners choose to draw on lines of equity, perhaps a home equity line. Remember, though, this is not free money. Even when interest rates are low on these lines of credit, you still will have incurred additional debt. Proceed carefully and consider interest payments when you plot your financial growth.

- *Venture capital.* This is private equity, typically provided by outside vendors. Venture capitalists tend to invest in higher risk businesses that have the potential for above-average returns. Most event planners will not rely on venture capital.

- *Banks.* You will be able to use your business plan to approach banks for loans, many geared specifically toward those creating a small business. It is imperative, when you approach a bank, that your business plan is thoughtful and thorough. Also, local banks are often more interested in financing small local businesses than larger, non-local chains.

- *Small Business Association.* Contact the Small Business Association (www.sba.com) for information about financing your developing small business.

If there is any single piece of advice most appropriate for the new entrepreneur in need of money, it is to make a careful assessment of the proposed value of the business, the amount of capital needed to finance it, in what increments it is needed, and the period of time you'll need the capital for. You'll need a business plan. You have made one, right? If not, go back to Chapter 2. (Do not pass GO. Do not collect $200. However, a good plan will help you collect a great deal more than that.)

Once you have your start-up money, it's time to go shopping for equipment.

Buying Equipment and Inventory

You'll need equipment and inventory for your company. In this section we'll discuss the must-haves and the nice-to-haves for event planners.

Before you go out and spend thousands of dollars, make a list, check it twice, and trim it well. Industry expert and author Patty Sachs advises new owners of event planning businesses to keep start-up costs low by buying only the minimum equipment and supplies. You need basic equipment, letterhead, business cards, a computer bookkeeping program, license or permit fees, internet service, and brochures or fliers to get you started. You will also need insurance, but you should not need inventory (e.g., party supplies). Lauren Polastri rents the party supplies she needs. And, says Kim Quigley, "We bought on an as-used basis."

Essential Equipment

Most event planners use standard office equipment such as copiers, fax machines, and computers. Many planners use meeting management software designed specifically for their field.

Small event planning businesses may not require much equipment. But no matter what the size of your business, invest in the following must-haves:

- *Vehicle.* You can use your own car, but you will need a vehicle for visiting clients and traveling to and from event sites. Using your own car will reduce the amount of start-up capital you need. Other options

Profile

Dallas planner Deborah K. Williams knows how to bargain. She found stellar deals on both rent and insurance rates. By renting in a then-unfashionable location and taking excellent care of the property, she gained a loyal landlord who locked in her rent at a low rate. Similarly, by giving all her insurance business to a small company, she saved a bundle. "I wheeled and dealed," she says.

are to lease or purchase a company vehicle. Remember, your car is a reflection of you and your business. Keep it tidy. Don't leave your brochures and paperwork strewn about.

- *Office furniture.* Good quality used furniture may be an option. You'll need a desk, chair, filing cabinets, and bookshelves. In fact, you may already own most of this equipment.

- *Cellular phone or pagers.* Cell phones have bcome an indispensable part of doing business in the event planning industry. Some entrepreneurs use their pager and cell phone together to save money. Make sure to buy a headset. Many states now mandate their use while driving.

- *Multiple phone lines.* One phone line is usually not enough. Install a multiline (push-button) phone system, allowing you to switch back and forth between lines while on one phone. In general, you'll need one phone line for every five employees (if you have any, that is). It is ideal to keep your work line and personal line separate. You will appear as more professional to prospective clients—you don't want your toddler answering your home line when a prospective client is on the other end. Having separate phone lines will help at tax time, as well, when it is time to deduct expenses.

- *Answering machine or voice mail.* You must provide a way for clients, vendors, and others to leave messages in your absence. Consider using music on your answering machine that reflects the tone of your business. These little touches add to your professional image.

- *Computer.* A computer is essential not only for producing professional-looking proposals, but also for keeping records and tracking information. It is a valuable time-saver to be able to pull up a proposal for a previous event, make the necessary adjustments and then send the revised proposal to the new client. A computer is also necessary for using the internet, a valuable tool for event planners.

- *E-mail and internet access.* E-mail and internet access are vital to your business. You'll be able to find vendors, research hotels and convention sites, network with other event planners and more in a quick and inexpensive fashion using your internet access. You will also be able to do market research as well as market your business. In other words, e-mail and internet access are absolutely indispensable.

- *Printer.* The ability to send out professional-looking proposals is important, and you'll need a printer to do that. Unless your business does very high-end events, however, a good inkjet printer should be fine. Make sure you pick one that is compatible with your computer.

How Does a Computer Really Work?

If you haven't used a computer often or are intimidated by the prospect of buying a new one for your new business, read on. Kathie Flood, Senior Program Manager, Microsoft Games Studios, demystifies computers and offers some sound and straightforward advice for understanding these complicated machines.

○ *CPU: Central Processing Unit*. The CPU is your computer's brain, which can do thousands of different things per second. The speed of the CPU is measured in megahertz (MHz) or gigahertz (GHz) and should be no less than 1 or 1.2 GHz to run most common programs like Microsoft Office and Intuit QuickBooks. Many new computers have a dual processor, which is especially fast and efficient, i.e., improves battery life on a laptop.

○ *RAM: Random Access Memory*. RAM is your computer's short-term memory or virtual scratch pad. RAM is measured in megabytes (MB or megs, 1 million bytes) or gigabytes (GB or gigs, 1 billion bytes). More RAM enables your computer to run more complex programs. If your computer has at least 1 to 1.5 GB, you should be able to run most common programs smoothly and simultaneously.

○ *Hard Drive*. This is your computer's permanent storage space, which you can think of as long-term memory. Like RAM, hard-drive space is measured in megabytes (MB) or gigabytes (GB). However, because this is your computer's permanent storage space, you will need much more hard-drive space than RAM. You should have at least 40 to 60 GB to enable you to store the many photos, videos, and documents you will accumulate while running your business.

○ *CD or DVD Drive*. This is the device that plays CDs and/or DVDs. Many CD and DVD drives are also capable of writing to blank CDs and DVDs. Writeable CDs and DVDs are very useful for creating discs that contain documents, photos, and videos that are too big for e-mail or must be delivered via snail-mail or courier. You can also use writeable CDs and DVDs for small-scale backups.

○ *Operating System*. This is the program that enables you to tell your computer what to do. Most personal computers run Microsoft Windows as their operating system (Vista is the most current version), but there are others, such as Apple OS-X and Linux.

○ *Ethernet Port, Wireless Internet Card, and/or Modem*. These are all used to connect your computer to the outside world. An ethernet port is where you would plug a cable for direct network access. A wireless internet card also provides network access, but without a cable. A modem enables you to connect a network or to send a fax via a telephone line.

- *Digital camera.* The ability to show clients your work online can be valuable. However, a traditional camera might be sufficient if you have a good scanner or have the photos put on a disc when they are developed. Digital cameras carry a wide price range, from $150 to $550.

- *Software.* Virus-detection software, as described earlier, is a necessity, and you must update it regularly.

There are five main types of software you may need: a word-processing program, a spreadsheet program, a relational database, desktop publishing software, and specialty software.

There are many software programs available now. We provide only a few examples here. For more information about software, consult the web sites provided in our Appendix.

> **Smart Tip** *Tip...*
>
> Make developing a company logo a priority. Part of creating a business is about developing a brand image. We all recognize McDonald's golden arches and Nike's swoosh. Although design software, such as InDesign, makes it possible for a novice to create a logo, it is often better to pay a graphic designer for this service. You want your logo to be professional, memorable, and unique. Don't opt for a clip art logo. These can look tacky and may show up on another planner's marketing materials. Finally, make sure your logo appears on everything, from your business cards to your web site.

1. *Word processing program.* Allows you to write text. Used for writing evaluations, forms, letters, lists, and anything else you want to write. Most planners we spoke to use Microsoft Word. Make sure you have a recent version (approximately $200).

2. *Spreadsheet program.* Helps you manipulate numbers. Used for producing outlines, schedules, timelines, budgets, and calendars, among other uses. Excel (about $200) is often cited by event planners, as is Quicken. The latter costs anywhere from $40, for the most basic version, to $60 for a more luxurious version.

3. *Relational database.* Allows you to manage, update, and use information from other databases. Used to produce name badges, receipts, reports, tickets, etc. If you are planning only small events, you may not need this type of software. If you choose to buy meeting management software, you will want to do some research. Ask other planners what type of software they use. With hundreds of varieties of software on the market—with price points ranging from $100 to thousands of dollars—you will have to determine which software works best for your company and best services the types of events you plan. For complete reports on 170 software products, consider buying *The Ultimate Meeting Professionals Software Guide*, available at www.mpiweb.org at a cost of $35. This guide details each software's strengths as weaknesses as well as offering price information.

4. *Desktop publishing*. Gives your products a polished look. Used for name badges, posters, press releases, signage, tickets, etc. Microsoft Publisher ($150) is a good starting point.

5. *Specialty software*. Allows you to perform specific tasks. Used for name badges, place cards, signage, tickets, diagrams, floor plans, etc. For example, room design software lets you design floor plans for meetings. Once you enter the room's dimensions, you can place elements such as walls, doors, and seats in various arrangements until you reach the best one for your event. You may find that all of your specialty software needs are met through your other software, such as your meeting management software. As a new business developer, you probably do not need to worry too much about buying specialty software. As your company grows and you determine a need for this software, then make a decision to buy.

> ## Tip...
>
> ### Smart Tip
> Create a database of all your vendor information, including products/services, prices, policies, and delivery times. By having this information computerized and retrievable within seconds, you will drastically reduce your time and work. Back up this data on your computer or on a disc and make sure you also have a Rolodex or some other hard copy of the list, in event of a computer failure.

There are many other items you might need. If you have a larger business, some of the following equipment items may be necessities. For smaller companies, these may fall into the nice-to-have category.

- *Walkie-talkies*. Jaclyn Bernstein and her employees often use walkie-talkies to communicate on the job. You can buy a basic walkie-talkie for $40; a high-end one will cost $150.

- *Laminating machine*. Bernstein also has a laminating machine to make signage for the events her business produces. Cost of this equipment ranges from $50 to $250.

- *Typewriter*. Handy for filling out forms, a typewriter may also help you out of a temporary computer emergency.

- *Copier*. If your company makes more than a few hundred copies per month or if you don't have time to keep running out for copies, you should consider investing in a copier to save time spent going to the copy shop. For $300 to $500, you can buy a multifunction machine that combines the functions of printer/copier/fax machine.

- *Scanner*. This piece of equipment is occasionally handy to have, but it's not essential for event planners. If you don't already have one, you're probably better off buying a digital camera so you can avoid scanning your photos into your web site. If you do buy a scanner, you'll note a large quality/price range. The simplest scanner costs about $50, and the most deluxe one, capable of scanning not only documents and large stacks of photos but also slides and negatives, is about $300. Some printers come equipped with scanners as well as copying capabilities.

- *Fax machine.* Most entrepreneurs benefit from being able to fax documents to clients. You will probably be able to fax from your computer.

Tracking Inventory

Some planners store an inventory of decorations and props. However, most rent these as needed, especially large items like gazebos and arches. You must consider both the storage space requirements and the maintenance requirements of inventory, as both will affect your overhead costs. Remember, unless you store only very small, low-maintenance items, you'll need more space and employee (or your own) time devoted to inventory upkeep. And no matter what kind of inventory you stock, you'll have to spend time tracking it.

How many smaller inventory items (e.g., centerpiece items, candles, etc.) should you stock? That depends in large part on whether you handle event decor yourself or contract it out to a designer or decorator. Most of the event planners we talked to hire vendors to provide decor. Therefore, they stock very little inventory. And so should you, at least at the beginning. As a rule, you should buy items as you need them. Most planners we talked to had no start-up inventory costs at all.

So what do planners routinely keep as inventory? Those we interviewed listed the following items:

- *Photos and videos.* Most planners keep photos of events their companies have produced. This industry is a very visual

one. "People want to see what you've done," says David Granger. Many planners put photos on their web sites as well as use them in portfolios and keep them in resource cabinets. Photos are also vital when producing proposals to present to clients.

- *Vendor catalogs and brochures.* Joyce Barnes-Wolff has several resource cabinets filled with these. Well-chosen catalogs and brochures are a good source of ideas and valuable reference aids for unusual items.

- *Gifts.* Several planners stock gifts for clients. Jaclyn Bernstein keeps a variety. Martin Van Keken stocks gifts of silver-plated yo-yos with the company logo.

Beware!
Don't forget less obvious costs. These can include, but are not restricted to, items such as the following: association memberships, subscriptions to industry publications, professional photography services, small promotional gifts, a new-business open house, custom colors for special print pieces, professional portfolio creation, van rental for transporting larger equipment, and T-shirts or uniforms for your hired helpers for larger events.

- *Fabric.* Fabric accounts for most of Martin Van Keken's inventory. He has an extensive collection, upon which he relies heavily. David Granger keeps three-ring binders of linen swatches. Some planners, like Jaclyn Bernstein, own table linens.

- *Floral containers.* Most planners keep containers for floral arrangements. These include urns, wrought-iron stands, and bowls for floating arrangements, besides the more traditional vases. Williams, Quigley, and Granger rent plants and other items as part of their business. Their table-top décor ranges from statuary items to antique hat boxes. If you use a florist or greenhouse, however, your floral-container needs will be minimal.

- *Lighting.* Most planners either rent lights or hire a lighting company. And they buy candles for specific events.

Our suggestion about equipment also holds true for inventory: Buy only what you need to get started. Most items should be acquired on a per-event basis. To make sure you are ready to start up, fill in the checklist on page 78.

Once you have bought the required equipment, inventory, and other supplies for your event planning business, it's time to consider hiring the help you'll need.

Start-Up Checklist

Equipment

❑ Vehicle

❑ Office furniture

❑ Phone

❑ Phone line(s)

❑ Answering machine or voice mail

❑ Cellular phone/pager

❑ Computer

❑ Printer

❑ Scanner

❑ Digital camera

❑ Software (general)

❑ Software (event planning)

❑ E-mail/internet access

❑ Web site

❑ Fax machine

❑ Copier

❑ Typewriter

❑ Laminating machine

❑ Walkie-talkies

Inventory/Miscellaneous

❑ Vendor catalogs

❑ Client gifts

❑ Fabric

❑ Floral containers

❑ Lighting

❑ Misc. (office supplies)

❑ Misc. (write in)

The
Fundamentals
of Hiring
Employees

Even if you plan to develop an event planning business focusing primarily on small social events, you will still find it necessary, at times, to hire help. You will likely want to hire temporary employees to help with specific events. Larger event planners will opt to hire permanent employees.

Event Planning News

All of the event planners interviewed for this guide are seeing growth in anniversary parties, particularly golden and silver anniversary fetes. Not only are the planners seeing more parties but also more elaborate parties. Gone, say the planners, are the days of the punch bowl and coffee urn. Today's celebrants are opting for grander locales and lush displays of food. Note, too, that if you are planning a golden anniversary event, the celebrants are entitled to a note from the current U.S. President. Simply e-mail the White House at www.comments@whitehouse.gov.

Choosing employees—whether temporary or permanent—can be a deal maker, or breaker, for your growing company. "The single most important thing to succeed," stresses Martin Van Keken, "is to create a very, very reliable team around you."

The planners we interviewed for this guide had anywhere from 0 to 12 permanent employees. Lauren Polastri hires temporary help as necessary. Because she lives in an area near the shore, her business booms during summer months. During these busy times, she takes on temporary employees.

Deborah Williams and Kim Quigley did not hire any permanent employees for the first three years. Their company now has 11, counting themselves. Joyce Barnes-Wolff, however, prefers a smaller company, with only herself and an assistant as permanent employees.

All planners—even those with permanent staffs in place—hire temporary personnel, often in large numbers, on an as-needed basis. For example, Vancouver planner Martin Van Keken, whose company has 12 permanent employees, hires anywhere from 10 to 150 temporary employees, depending on the size and complexity of the event. As is the case for Lauren Polastri, you might live in an area with well-defined on- and off-seasons. If this is the case, then you will need to hire staff during busy or peak times. Part-time employees may help set up and tear down an event site. They might also be servers or ushers. Part-time workers are ideal for office tasks such as entering data into the computer and addressing and mailing envelopes.

Someone, whether yourself, a permanent staff member, or a temporary employee, will be needed to fill each of the following roles:

- *Office manager*: oversees and coordinates employees and may also handle administrative, clerical, and office-supply duties
- *Planner*: helps plan events
- *Sales staff*: sells events to clients; networks to gain additional business
- *Designer*: handles decor if you do not hire vendors to do that
- *Public relations representative*: handles public relations involving clients, vendors, suppliers, and the general public

- *Director of marketing*: takes charge of advertising and promotion; often, the public relations representative and the director of marketing are the same person
- *Bookkeeper*: tracks all business and per-event expenses, and may also prepare tax returns; if you hire an accountant to do these tasks, you may not need a book-keeper
- *On-site assistant*: helps set up and tear down at the event site
- *Setup staff*: greets guests, helps run registration or concession stands, serves food and/or drinks
- *Craft services staff*: provides help with craft items, preparation of invitations, etc.
- *Kitchen staff*: cleans up
- *Gofer*: runs errands
- *Driver*: delivers supplies to the venue

Note that the above list is about roles, not titles. There is considerable variety in titles given to employees, but whether you use informal titles or more formal ones (e.g., production coordinator, account manager, operations assistant), the tasks are the same.

Don't be alarmed by the length of this list. You do not need to hire a separate employee for each of these duties. Rather, you may choose to fulfill all or most of these duties yourself.

Tip...

Smart Tip

When hiring employees, consider the types of benefits you will be able to offer. These are an important incentive when choosing employees, as you will tend to field a better applicant pool if you offer benefits, including paid vacation, sick days, personal days, flexible work schedules, trips to professional conferences, company-funded professional training, and health insurance, for instance. Joyce Barnes-Wolff joined the local chamber of commerce to provide benefits for her employees. "I needed insurance I could not afford on an individual basis," she says. "It's more affordable as a member." Benefits come at a price, though. Full-time employees will cost you between 15 percent and 30 percent above their wages or salaries, depending on the benefits you offer.

Reaching Out to Candidates

Once you have determined the type of positions you will need to fill, you will need to advertise these open positions. Don't skimp on this step. Simply put, you want to cast your net as widely as possible to garner the best employees.

Advertising. Consider placing an advertisement in your local and regional newspapers. If the job you are filling is a more senior-level position, then also consider advertisements in larger newspapers as well as trade journals. These national ads, though,

Tell It Like It Is

When you decide it is time to hire employees, write a clear and detailed job description that outlines the objectives of the job (while you're at it, write your own job description—this will help you to delegate and assign job descriptions to others). Use bulleted points to target the responsibilities of the position, the working conditions, and the relationships of the position to other jobs. Also clearly delineate the ideal candidate's skill set. This is critical because when you interview prospective candidates, these will act as a type of checklist. It is tempting to hire employees that you immediately like, but do not necessarily have the strongest skills. Try not to let emotion take over when hiring employees. Of course, it is important that you and your employees' working styles mesh. As New York City planner Jaclyn Bernstein puts it, "You have to be friends when you work crazy hours with these people." Remember, too, to hire qualified candidates.

will be much more expensive, so plan on placing national ads only when the position warrants. Employment ads are typically placed in the classified section. Call your local paper and ask for an advertising representative who can walk you through the options. You may choose a simple three-line ad, or select a splashier, larger ad with a border helping to draw readers' attention. Be specific about your needs: hours, responsibilities, pay range, benefits, and qualities the applicant must possess (e.g. previous event planning experience). Finally, make sure no words are misspelled in this ad. Sounds simple, but, too often, classified ads make their way into print filled with typos. This will make you look less than professional. Run spell check and make sure everything is in tip top spelling shape.

- *Online advertising.* Check with the advertising representative at your local paper to see if the newspaper offers an online option. Most newspapers offer packages, including print only, online only, or both types of advertising. If the newspaper offers an online option, plan on placing an online as well as print version of your advertisement.

- *Craigslist.org.* This online advertising site is booming with more and more event planners turning to it to find employees.

- *Colleges and universities.* Colleges and universities often have their own newspapers as well as web sites on which you can post your job openings. This is an excellent source for finding able candidates, especially for less senior positions.

- *Word-of-mouth.* Like so many other aspects of the event planning industry, word-of-mouth often proves invaluable in finding key employees. Let your

Beware! Although it might be tempting to take up your mother's offer to help staff your growing business, these arrangements too often end in misunderstandings, with mom, perhaps, feeling she is underappreciated. If you do choose to work with friends or family, treat this as a professional arrangement and pay them as you would other employees.

vendors and other event planners know that you are looking for employees. Get the word out and you will start hearing about candidates who might be suitable for your company.

Interviewing Applicants

As you begin hearing from prospective applicants, you will want to read through their resumes and create a point system, perhaps from 1 to 10, giving 1's to unqualified candidates and 10's to top candidates. You shouldn't have many 1's (if you wrote an apt job description, unqualified applicants aren't likely to apply) nor 10's (dream candidates are, as the name implies, rare). As you survey the resumes, use your rating system to decide which applicants to interview.

Interviewing Strategies

Plan on interviewing five to ten applicants for more senior positions, fewer for less senior spots. When an applicant arrives for an interview, have her complete an application form. These are available at local business supply stores such as Staples. You'll want to ask all candidates the same series of questions, ensuring a fair process. For help in formulating these questions, check www.job-interview.net. This site offers tips and advice about job interviewing and appropriate questions.

Take notes during interviews so you can review your notes later and winnow these candidates to two finalists. Ask these two for a second interview. Again, ensure fairness by asking both candidates the same series of questions. Take notes so you can access responses of both candidates after the interviews and make a final selection.

After the second interview, you will need to write an offer letter to the winning candidate, laying out your proposal, complete with pay structure and benefits. Once you and the applicant have signed the letter, you should let the other finalist know that the position is filled. Wait until the winning applicant has formally accepted before letting the losing candidate know the bad news. Too many times, the winning candidate has to decline the offer. Perhaps, she received another offer and is unable to take the job. If this is the case, you will need to turn to your second candidate.

Always keep all candidates apprised of your time frame for hiring and let them know when to expect news. Always follow through, including making the tough calls, letting candidates know when they aren't selected.

Paying Your Employees

There are many variables to consider when paying your staff. For instance, in more urban areas of the country, pay tends to be higher. Compensation is also based on the employee's experience level and amount of responsibility. An inexperienced worker with only moderate responsibilities makes anywhere from $18,000 to $32,000. An experienced employee with heavy responsibility probably makes between $25,000 and $45,000.

If you hire temporary help in coordinating an event, industry expert Patty Sachs says, the average wage is $10 to $15 per hour for setup staff. Craft services staff make $8 to $10 per hour.

You can pay other temporary or part-time employees either hourly or per event. They usually earn $8 to $10 per hour. If you decide to pay your intern (which will make attracting one easier), consider an hourly wage between $8 and $10 per hour or offering a stipend, i.e., a flat amount compensating the intern for a specific amount of time, usually for the duration of the semester. Stipends can range from $500 to $1000 per semester. If your intern is a graduate student trained in some facet of event planning, you should expect to pay anywhere from $12 to $15 per hour, depending on responsibilities and, again, on the area of the country. If you live in an urban area where teenage baby sitters command $15 an hour, then you can count on paying your hourly staffers a higher-than-average hourly stipend.

Training Time

Be a good boss and take the time to adequately train your new hires. There is simply nothing more frustrating for a new employee than being left to founder. Spend the time needed to train your new hires and they will quickly get up to speed. Plan on providing each employee with a detailed job description, delineating his or her responsibilities. Clarity and open lines of communication are key when dealing with employees.

Bright Idea

If a local college offers courses in event management or related areas (e.g., travel and tourism, hotel management), part-time employees and interns should be easy to find. Contact the head of the department and ask about the internship program. Local chapters of industry associations such as ISES and MPI may also offer internship referrals. And you can look on the web (see the Appendix).

Choosing Vendors

At the heart of a successful event planner's business is a team of reliable vendors. It can't be overstated: your events will be marred by even one bad vendor. Just as a bad apple ruins the lot, one bad vendor may leave a bad image in your client's mind of the event as a whole. Perhaps the florist arrives with wilted and faded centerpieces. It's hard to erase this image from the minds of both your client as well as the minds of attendees. You must do your due diligence when it comes to finding top-rate vendors.

Types of Vendors

- *Art director*: handles design, computer imaging, etc.
- *Caterer/bartender*: serves food and beverages
- *Calligrapher*: handles lettering on invitations and signage
- *Decorator*: provides decor
- *Florist*: provides floral arrangements
- *Graphic artist*: designs and executes event posters or invitations
- *Photographer/videographer*: photographs, records, and preserves the event
- *Performer*: provides entertainment
- *Transportation/parking personnel*: drives and parks vehicles

Bright Idea

Remember, you are working in a "fun" industry that often involves celebration. Consider a weekly, or monthly office celebration. Bring in something simple, like cookies or doughnuts. Anything of this nature improves office morale. Consider a monthly themed celebration. These events don't need to be fancy. A themed breakfast could be as simple as providing pirate hats, eye patches, and doughnuts for a festive "Pirates of the Caribbean" morning kick-off.

If you want a good motto to do business by, consider one of author and industry consultant Patty Sachs': "Don't Wait—Celebrate!"

Finding the A-List Suppliers

As outlined above, even if a mistake is a vendor's fault, the mishap will reflect on you because you are managing the event. That's what makes researching vendors so important. David Granger picks his with extreme care. "Choosing vendors means knowing them and trusting them," he says. As do most event planners, Jaclyn Bernstein makes her choices with long-term relationships in mind. She has even had business come her way through vendors who know her.

Joyce Barnes-Wolff has "the best Rolodex in the Midwest," she says. So she knows who's right for an event. "I can pull in the best people from across the area."

Martin Van Keken places extreme importance on vendor selection. "They're part of our team," he says.

All of the event planners interviewed for this book cautioned against letting your fingers do the walking when it comes to finding the best vendors. The best idea, successful event planners say, is to ask questions and listen carefully to the answers. Ask other event planners and clients about their experiences with vendors. The names of the best—and worst—vendors will be

Beware!

Before you hire any vendors, make sure they carry the proper insurance (see Chapter 4) and meet any other legal requirements. A valet-parking service, for instance, needs to be insured, and perhaps bonded, in case a valet damages a car while he or she parks it. A caterer needs a food-handling permit and insurance. Even entertainers may need to carry insurance.

Inside Out

In their book, *The Art of Event Design* (Primedia Business Magazines & Media Inc.), authors Liese Gardner and Susan Terpening point out several benefits of working with individuals from outside the special events industry. Not only is this a good way to add style and distinction to the events you plan, such a strategy can also be a money saver. Consider the following possibilities:

○ *Art students.* You can end up with interesting and inexpensive centerpieces if you get art students to make them for you. Check out the art department at the nearest college or university. Also take a look at the theater department if you need costumes or a backdrop for an event. Sometimes rentals are possible.

○ *Art dealers.* See if you can rent paintings for an event.

○ *Music students.* Need a pianist for an event? Consider the nearest school of music. Many students studying for master's degrees or doctorates will perform for a fraction of the cost of hiring a professional.

○ *Window dressers.* Go window shopping and find out who designed the displays you admire. That individual may make an excellent decor consultant for you.

These are only a few of many possibilities. Use your imagination! But because these individuals may not have their own insurance, make sure you have coverage for anyone on-site during the event.

mentioned again and again. Keep a list of both those that are recommended and those with tarnished reputations. With these lists in hand, start researching the vendors on your A-list, recording the following information:

- Vendor name, address, contact information
- Area of service
- Prices
- Lead times required
- Payment policy
- Refund policy
- Discounts offered
- Specialty items/services
- Insurance coverage
- Types of licenses and permits held

This vendor file is extremely important because it can save you hours of research time down the road, Sachs says. By having all this information right at your fingertips, you'll be able to conduct your vendor searches more effectively. Keep building this file as each new event comes along. A computerized file can be even more of a time saver.

Before you hire a vendor for the first time, find out all you can about the company's history. Ask for letters of reference, too. Or, ask if you can attend an event at which the vendor is providing a service. Once you are satisfied, make sure you have a document indicating what the company will do for your event. Vendor proposals should include the following elements:

- Complete description of service
- Description of equipment vendor will provide
- Listing of additional services vendor will provide, if any
- Description of costs and payment terms
- Scheduling information
- Proof of insurance, bonding, and other risk-management practices
- List of vendor requirements (water, electricity, etc.)

Beware!

Food and beverages, and the servers that go along with them, are an important part of most special events. In fact, the catering bill often accounts for 40 percent of an event's budget. So pay special attention to choosing the caterer. Ask what the company's specialties are. Also ask to sample every item from the event menu before signing the contract. Many event planners join the National Association of Catering Professionals, finding it a terrific avenue for networking and finding reliable catering professionals.

In addition, make sure these details all appear in the vendor agreement (see Chapter 4 on page 65).

Negotiating with Vendors

There are some points on which you can negotiate when hiring vendors, especially as your experience and reputation grow. As a general rule, the more often you have worked with vendors, the more leeway you can reasonably expect them to accord you. Consider asking about the following:

- *Payment terms*. Get your required deposit as low as possible. Also, ask about a prepayment (i.e., paying in full before the event) discount.
- *Complimentary sample* (e.g., food-tasting). This point is especially important either when hiring a vendor unknown to you or when you are asking for something outside the vendor's normal style of service.
- *Complimentary extra*. When you provide a lot of business for vendors, they may be persuaded to throw in something at no charge. For example, a florist who provides centerpieces and other floral arrangements for a large event may provide a free bouquet for the guest of honor.

Hiring Professional Help

You will, at times, need to hire professionals for consultations. Although these services sometimes arrive with a rather steep price tag, it is absolutely money well spent. These professionals will help to ensure the success of your event planning business.

Professional consultants with whom event planners may work include:

- *Accountant*. A good accountant will be your single most important outside advisor and will have the greatest impact on the success or failure of your event planning business. You will have to decide if your volume warrants a full-time book-keeper, an outside accounting service, or merely a year-end accounting and tax-preparation service. Even the smallest unincorporated event planning businesses employ outside public accountants to prepare their financial statements. All

Dollar Stretcher

If you plan on doing most of your bookkeeping and are looking primarily for tax help, consider hiring an enrolled agent rather than an accountant. They can be found in the Yellow Pages or through the National Association of Enrolled Agents (www.naea.org).

planners interviewed for this book told us they have an accountant. Accountants typically charge $75 to $150 per hour.

- *Attorney.* Finding the right lawyer early is critical. Make sure you hire an attorney you can trust and be comfortable with. You may need your lawyer to help ensure that your business is in compliance with licensing and insurance regulations. A lawyer can also check documents before you sign them and help you draft documents like vendor and client agreements. And, of course, an attorney will help resolve any legal problems that may arise. However, do not wait until you have legal difficulties before hiring a lawyer. Attorney's fees range from $100 to $500 per hour.

- *Business consultant.* You may consider hiring a professional to analyze your business plan and check your ideas for feasibility. A good consultant can keep you from making costly mistakes.

- *Event planning consultant.* This individual can help you with all stages of planning an event. If you are new to the industry, consider hiring a seasoned planner whose niche does not overlap with yours.

- *Banker.* The right banker can be a tremendous asset to an event planner. Sometimes, in spite of contracts, clients (especially large corporations) do not pay their deposits on time, says Jaclyn Bernstein. Event planners, however, have to pay vendor deposits. This problem can create a financial crunch for

Choosing a Lawyer

Consider these factors when choosing an attorney:

- ❍ Will the attorney meet with you in person for an initial consultation—rather than a phone consultation?
- ❍ What is the attorney's background and experience? Specialty? Length of time in practice?
- ❍ Does the attorney have other event planners as clients?
- ❍ Will the lawyer or paralegals perform the bulk of the work?
- ❍ Is there a charge for the initial consultation?
- ❍ What is the charge for routine legal work?
- ❍ Will the attorney work on a contingency basis?
- ❍ Is the attorney's web site professional and appealing to you?
- ❍ Always check with your state bar association as well (www.abanet.org).

you. However, a banker who has a good, long-standing relationship with your company may "float" you the required funds. "You need a good banker in this business," she says.

- *Insurance broker.* Another professional you will rely on is your insurance broker. Get one who will work with you. If you buy several types of insurance from the same company, you should receive a more attractive deal on the package. Deborah Williams gave all her business to a small insurance company and saved well over 50 percent on her liability insurance.

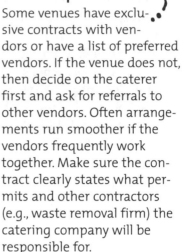

Smart Tip

Some venues have exclusive contracts with vendors or have a list of preferred vendors. If the venue does not, then decide on the caterer first and ask for referrals to other vendors. Often arrangements run smoother if the vendors frequently work together. Make sure the contract clearly states what permits and other contractors (e.g., waste removal firm) the catering company will be responsible for.

Remember, investigate well and give careful thought to hiring those who will work with you. The time you invest in choosing your employees and other professionals will pay off in the end as you create a solid, smoothly running team for your business.

Once you have your team, it's time to get the word out! Chapter 7 focuses on how to advertise and market your services and how to improve your customer service.

Marketing Your
Business

As you develop your business, it is impor-
tant to market to and grow your client base. The planners interviewed for this guide offered varied marketing models. Some
successful planners rely solely on word of mouth promotion,
noting that nothing can compare to a referral from a previous
client. Others maintain informative web sites or offer their

▲

Developing a SWOT Analysis

Before you begin advertising and marketing in earnest, develop a road map of your marketing plans. This plan should include a SWOT analysis. SWOT stands for:

○ *Strengths*. It is always useful to focus on this question. What are the unique and particular strengths of your business? How do these strengths set you apart from the competition?

○ *Weaknesses*. Be honest—even if it hurts! What areas of your business are weak? Develop strategies to combat these weaknesses.

○ *Opportunities*. As the name implies, these are things that might benefit your company, now or in the future. For instance, perhaps a new convention center is opening in your area. This is an opportunity for you to grow your business.

○ *Threats*. List anything that might harm your business. Perhaps, a corporate presence is closing its doors and relocating. Or, a new event planner is hanging out her shingle.

By focusing on these four areas and writing about them, you will help to focus your marketing efforts.

client base a weekly e-mail newsletter. As your company grows, you will determine which model works best. The pace at which you would like your company to grow will determine this, in part. Lauren Polastri had relied solely on word-of-mouth marketing as she purposefully developed a small company, a size she chose so she could also be available for her young children. Now she is ready to move to the next level so is planning to place an ad in her local Yellow Pages.

In this chapter we'll provide suggestions to guide you though the process of developing your strategy and help you evaluate the advertising media commonly used in the event planning industry. We'll also look at several other ways you can promote yourself and your new business.

Networking to Business Success

Virtually every planner interviewed for this guide places networking at the top of their list in terms of developing a strong client base.

Dr. Joe Goldblatt, CSEP, founding director of the Event Management Program at George Washington University, explains that networking can prove more effective—and almost always less expensive—than traditional print advertising.

Dallas planner David Granger agrees. The problem, he notes, is that customers need to see what you do, and a word ad won't accomplish that. He recommends networking and making friends in the industry. That way, he says, "People know you, trust you. They want honesty and integrity."

Likewise, industry expert and veteran planner John Daly doesn't use traditional advertising. He networks. He's active in industry organizations like National Association of Catering Executives (NACE) and International Special Events Society (ISES).

Networking can help your business in two ways. If people have met you and know what services you offer, they may refer business to you or use your service themselves. Furthermore, networking with hotels, caterers, and so on will give you a chance to meet some of the people whose services you may need as you plan events.

The In's and Out's of Advertising

Print advertising covers a broad range, from a free—or inexpensive—Yellow Pages advertisement to an ad in a glossy national publication costing tens of thousands of dollars.

Most planners agree that an ad in the Yellow Pages makes good business sense. A line advertisement, simply listing your business name, is often provided free of charge when you connect your phone. You can also opt for a display advertisement. These are the bigger, bordered ads in the Yellow Pages. There is a charge for these. If you do choose a larger ad space, be sure to include your logo. Also, be aware of the publication cycle of your local phone book. If you open your business in June, but the directory isn't published until January of the following year, you will need to look elsewhere to promote your business.

You may also want to consider advertising in your local newspaper. Many papers periodically (perhaps quarterly) publish special sections for brides- and grooms-to-be. These are good vehicles for promoting your event planning business if you plan to do any wedding consulting.

Regional magazines can be useful if you plan both corporate and social occasions. Because the market area for this kind of event planner can extend throughout a given county, a magazine focusing on that county can be an excellent one in which to advertise. These magazines can be geared to topics related to your service (e.g., gourmet food, floral design) or aimed at readers in a certain region. An ad in a regional magazine might be a good tool for reaching upscale consumers. A regional business magazine ad would reach prospective corporate clients.

▲

Advertising in national publications will not pay off for most planners since the cost is simply too prohibitive. Instead, target your advertising dollars on the client base closer to your home.

Your Business Card, Small but Mighty

Don't underestimate the power of this small but mighty marketing tool. Consider it a diminutive brochure, especially if you opt for a tri-fold business card. Many planners opt for this business-card format because more information can be included than on a traditional business card, while the card remains small enough to be tucked inside a wallet or purse.

Include the name of your business, contact information (e-mail, phone, fax, and web site address, for instance), your name, specialization, your logo, and some testimonials from past clients. Always check with clients before using their testimonials and ask for permission to use both their first and last names. Testimonials signed by John D. or Jane S. just don't have the same impact as those signed with a full name.

Always carry business cards. You might stand behind someone in the grocery store, strike up a conversation, and discover that she is starting to plan a bar mitzvah. This is the perfect opportunity to pass along your business card. Ask vendors with whom you work (florists, caterers, and photographers, for instance), if you can leave a stack of business cards in their places of business.

With business supply stores such as Staples and Office Max, printing business cards is a relatively inexpensive task. Choose the best stock (paper) you can afford. Likewise, if you are able to print in more than one color, then do so. For many clients, this will be their first impression of you and your business. Make sure it has a professional impact!

The Informative Brochure

Like your business card, a well-designed, professional brochure can help cement your image as a professional planner. Prospective clients will make judgments about your company based on your brochure so make sure that it is conceived and produced at the highest level possible.

Smart Tip

Tip...

As you develop strategies for advertising and marketing your company, remember that your company logo must appear on every marketing piece—from your tri-fold business card to the home page of your web site. This helps prospective clients to remember you and your corporate image. If you haven't had a logo designed yet, now is the time!

> ## Beware!
>
> If you decide to try direct mail, don't try to use your mailing list more than once. These lists are "seeded" with control names so the list seller will know if you use the list more than once. Also, make sure you acquire your mailing list from a business in a related industry (e.g., party supply shop, costume shop). This strategy will help target those potential clients most likely to use your services. Also, analyze the direct mailings you receive. What works, and what doesn't?

To achieve this, plan on hiring a free-lance graphic designer to help you develop this marketing tool. Tri-fold brochures are popular and allow you to include important information about your business. The brochure should include all of the information listed on your tri-fold business card and allow you to expand upon this information, in particular, by adding photographs. The photos should be of successful events you've designed. You may also want to include a photo of yourself. Because this marketing piece is making a critical first-impression on prospective clients, consider hiring a professional photographer to help you obtain first-rate photos.

Maximize your chances of success by making sure your company brochure matches the type of business you have. All materials should look professional, but unless you have a high-end event planning company, a too-glamorous brochure can send the wrong message—and send potential budget-conscious clients running in the opposite direction.

As with your business cards, leave your brochure with caterers, florists, photographers, and other vendors with whom you've worked. Provide the vendor with a brochure rack (available at Staples and other office supple stores) so your brochures don't end up in a messy stack on the floor somewhere—not professional!

Direct Mail

You may choose to distribute your brochure via direct mail. If you do so, make sure that your mailing list is well chosen. David Granger says that while word-of-mouth is their most effective advertising, Designs Behind the Scenes uses mailing lists of the organizations they belong to (ISES, MPI, NACE, and the Dallas Convention and Visitors Bureau).

Newsletters

Newsletters, if written in a lively and entertaining fashion, are useful marketing tools. Mail your newsletter to prospective, current, and previous clients, focusing on what is new in your business. Perhaps, you have expanded your services or are offering a specially-priced package. Keep the articles pithy and useful. Bulleted points are helpful to your client as are break-out boxes. Your clients' time is at a premium so keep the articles brief.

You may choose to send your newsletter via e-mail, an inexpensive and effective alternative to the slower "snail mail." Be sure your client wants to receive the newsletter via e-mail. You don't want to be accused of sending spam!

Press Releases

Sending press releases is a fantastic and inexpensive method by which to boost your business. Send releases when you have business news to report—perhaps you have changed locations, planned your 1,000th event, or have some other event that is newsworthy. Newspaper and magazine editors need this so-called news "hook," so don't send press releases without news content. Editors won't run these.

A press release should include:

- *Release date*. Unless your release shouldn't be printed right away, then write "For Immediate Release" at the top.
- *Contact name*. Include your name, e-mail, and phone number.
- *Headline*. Editors may change your headline but give them an idea of the release content with a to-the-point, accurate headline.
- *Dateline*. This is the city from which the release originates. So, if your business is in Des Moines, then you should write "DES MOINES" in uppercase type. It should be placed as the first word of type before the press release text begins.
- *Text*. This is your news. Make it interesting to the editor so she will run it!

Most magazines and newspapers prefer that press releases be submitted via e-mail so staff does not have to spend time typing in releases sent via regular mail.

Although the editor may not choose to run all of your releases, it is still worthwhile to e-mail them off periodically. One reason for this is that the editor may turn to you when she needs a news source for a story on event planning. Or, she may choose to use one of your releases as the framework for a feature story, which is a larger newspaper article.

Creating a Powerful Web Site

Just as you can access other companies' web sites for information about their products and services, you'll want prospective clients as well as your regular clients to find

Entering the Blogosphere

Blogs are gaining popularity at an amazing pace. Blogs are essentially online journals or newsletters, usually with more than one author. You may find blogs useful for networking, brainstorming, and simply commiserating with other event planners. These sites allow for a back-and-forth of ideas and frustrations. Check out www.thepartygoddess.com/blog to see what blogs are all about!

you in cyberspace, too. That means establishing your web site should be a high priority on your list of business start-up essentials.

Many of the planners we interviewed use their web sites to reach national and international client bases. Says event planner Jaclyn Bernstein, "Web sites are great for showing what your company does." However, she cautions that web sites can't show everything, and that few clients will hire a planner based solely on a web site.

As you create your web site, these are "must haves":

- Homepage
- "Contact Us" page
- "About Us" page
- Testimonials from past clients and vendors. Use names not initials after these quotes, if possible.
- Photos (make sure you have your clients' permission to run these)
- Your company's logo should appear on all of the pages of your web site

Although the prospect of creating your own web site may be daunting, it is possible for a non-techie to get the job done. There are many do-it-yourself web page kits on the market. You may, though, want to consider hiring a web page developer to create one for you.

Web Design 101

Your web site might be the first encounter a prospective client has with you and your business. Also, your web site is virtual advertising that's available on demand 24 hours per day. For these reasons, take time to carefully consider what you want your site to say and what sort of look and feel it should convey. In other words, if you are creating a business specializing in black-tie, high-touch events, then your web site should be formal and elegant to reflect this.

Spend time looking at other event planners' web sites, keeping a checklist of what you like and don't like about these web sites and incorporate these findings into your design plans. Choose colors, typefaces, and other stylistic elements that work on other web sites.

Plan to keep copy brief because many people find it annoying to have to keep scrolling down as they read. In addition, if the text runs onto too many screens, it's harder for the customer to print material from your web site.

Naming Your Web Site

Your web site has to have a unique name that will be used on the server it resides on. Using the name of your event planning business is usually your best choice, but another planner may already be using the name you've chosen. Domain names must be registered for a minimum of two years, after which you can renew them. The cost to register a name for two years is approximately $70. There are several companies that handle registration, but the best known is DOMAIN.com, which also allows you to register your name for five- or ten-year periods. The cost for these longer registrations is $30 and $25 per year, respectively.

Choosing a Web Host

You must select a service to host your web site. Examples of well-known web hosts include Microsoft Network and Prodigy, but there are many, many smaller hosts around the country.

Before choosing a web host, ask these questions:

- How often does the site go down?
- How long does it take to fix the site when it goes down?
- What is its customer support system?
- How many incoming lines does the server have?

Smart Tip

There is no quicker way to undermine your credibility than to maintain a sloppy web site. *Do not let your web site become outdated.* Nothing will turn a client off faster than finding outdated information on a web site. Also, be sure that words are not misspelled. Misspelled words reflect carelessness and a lack of professionalism.

- What is the server's experience with high traffic sites?
- How big is the server?

The price of web fame starts as low as $14.95 per month. Some of the hosts will also allow you to register your domain at the same time.

Maintaining Your Client Base

How do you keep clients coming back? By paying close attention to three crucial (and interwoven) aspects of your business: customer service, public relations, and company image.

Beware!
A brief word on ethics: Remember, save your promotion efforts for the right place and time. During an event is not the right time. As Vancouver planner Martin Van Keken points out, this is the client's event. "I have no right or authority to start promoting myself," he says. By the same token, do not allow your vendors to promote their companies at an event.

The Power of Customer Service

Any business owner—or customer, for that matter—knows the one essential ingredient in running a successful business: customer service. You can be hard working and dedicated, construct a flawless business plan, and have a bottomless source of financing, but if you don't keep customers satisfied and coming back, your event planning business will never succeed.

One of the best ways to keep customers coming back is to be constantly on the lookout for new ideas and for ways to improve the service you provide. Toward that goal, consider the following:

- Take a course (or even a series of courses) in event management
- Invest in an hour (or more) with an industry consultant
- Attend other events to study how they are produced
- Attend as many arts-related functions as possible (e.g., arts exhibits, theatrical performances) to gather ideas

Profile
Event planner Martin Van Keken of MVKA Productions in Vancouver feels strongly about the importance of service. When a client wonders if something is feasible, his company thoroughly investigates it. His team is always looking for the new and the different. "Just going out of our way isn't good enough," he says.

▲

- Join trade organizations (see "Organization's the Key" on page 101)
- Subscribe to at least one professional newsletter or journal

Giving Back to Your Community

Besides providing excellent customer service, earning (and keeping) the goodwill of clients and the community is important. Volunteering your company's help in planning charitable events will win you many friends in the community. And you are sure to gain loyal clients if you are willing to do the following:

- *"Go to the wall" for clients.* All the event planners we interviewed mentioned the need to "make it right," at all costs. This could involve anything from a planner's ability to handle last-minute emergencies to a willingness to "throw in" something extra for free, simply because the planner feels the event would be incomplete without it.

At Your Service

If you choose to volunteer your planning services, industry consultant Patty Sachs has some advice for you. First, be sure that the events are ones in which you want to specialize. If you want to focus on board meetings, don't volunteer to plan a birthday party—time spent researching balloon types is not going to help you. Also be sure that the events are high-profile, such as a charity ball or a meeting for members of your city's chamber of commerce. These are the types of events that will be attended by people who may become potential clients. Finally, Sachs says, make sure to get credit for your work—have the phrase "Event Planned by Jane Doe, Anytown, State" delicately yet prominently added to all fliers, invitations, and signs promoting the party, as well as all programs or other materials handed out at the event. If a press release regarding the event is mailed to the local newspaper, be sure you and your company are mentioned somewhere in the release. If the client doesn't intend to send out a press release, consider doing so yourself.

Keep in mind that although volunteering involves a lot of work for no obvious monetary gain, the payoff can be big in the long run. The contacts you make through these first few events will expand into a solid base of satisfied clients who can recommend an experienced, proven event planner to their friends, family, and business associates. Remember, many event planners give their initial clients big discounts in the beginning anyway, because they know it's unfair to charge full price for their inexperience.

- *Offer clients something they can't get elsewhere.* Many planners mentioned the original aspect of the work they do. More and more, clients want the "different" and "unusual."

- *Make clients feel valued.* Many planners mentioned gifts that they give to clients. These can include everything from cookies and other edibles to unusual decorative items to elaborate floral arrangements. Besides giving gifts, however, there are other ways to make sure clients know they are appreciated. A simple note with a personal message to convey thanks, congratulations, or birthday wishes can mean a lot, as can a phone call. Or, consider putting together a small album of photos from your client's event. Some planners also entertain clients for lunch or dinner.

- *Think less in terms of services and more in terms of problem solving.* Says Joyce Barnes-Wolf, "We try to listen to clients' needs and facilitate them within their budget. When you have budget restrictions, it forces you to become creative."

You're Only as Good as Your Last Event

Image—the way your company and its services are viewed by the public—is very important. Some event planners, therefore, will direct much of their advertising and

Organization's the Key

There are several large organizations that serve the special events industry. Most entrepreneurs we interviewed belong to ISES (International Special Events Society), NACE (National Association of Catering Executives), and MPI (Meeting Professionals International). Most also belong to their local convention and visitors bureau. Some belong to the Better Business Bureau as well.

The annual Special Event is the largest and highest profile industry trade show. It is put on every January by Primedia Business Magazines & Media Inc, publishers of *Special Events* magazine. This trade show attracts a couple of thousand attendees from around the world.

If you are planning small-scale events with a local focus, you can still benefit from attending the national (and international) conferences. In addition, investigate local and regional organizations in your area. Involvement in industry organizations can provide you with ideas, valuable learning experiences, and excellent ways to network and become known in the event planning industry.

promotion dollars toward building a good company image. You will have to decide how much you can afford to spend to establish, improve, and maintain your image. Increased revenues may be able to compensate for this expenditure.

Most important by far, however, is what your events say about your business. The quality of the events you produce is the most powerful shaper of your company's image and reputation.

Don't forget that small details also reflect on you and your company. Remember, Goldblatt cautions, "From the selection of vendors to the choice of brochure paper, every decision you make reflects your taste and company image."

8

Managing Your
Finances

In this chapter, you'll find the basic dos and don'ts for managing your business's money. We'll suggest ways to maintain good cash flow. You'll learn how to arrive at an accurate pricing of your services and how to figure the break-even point for your event planning business. We'll also provide a few tax tips.

Financial Statements

How you manage your financial assets may determine whether your business succeeds or fails. Your capital is not merely a collection of money and property, but a powerful business tool deserving your careful attention. Because going into business for yourself is such a risky proposition, this capital should yield a higher rate of return than an ordinary investment would. Making capital work for you requires careful management of your business, especially of your current and future assets.

Financial management is an area many small-business owners neglect. They get so caught up in the day-to-day running of their businesses that they fail to take a good look at where their money goes.

Keeping good records helps generate the financial statements that tell you exactly where you stand and what you need to do next. The key financial statements you need to understand and use regularly are:

Event Planning News

Event planners need to keep on top of trends when developing events. From going green (creating completely organic and environmentally friendly events), to the trend toward unusual and interesting ethnic foods, event planners do some of their research at their local magazine rack.

Check out which magazine sections are largest and which magazines are thickest. There has been a proliferation of magazines geared toward Generation Y, for instance. This is a market savvy group event planners can target and develop.

- *Profit and loss statement* (also called the P&L or the income statement). This statement illustrates how much your company is making or losing over a designated period—monthly, quarterly, or annually—by subtracting expenses from your revenue to arrive at a net result, which is either a profit or a loss.

- *Balance sheet.* A balance sheet is a table showing your assets, liabilities, and capital at a specific point. A balance sheet is typically generated monthly, quarterly, or annually when the books are closed.

- *Cash flow statement.* This summarizes the operating, investing, and financing activities of your business as they relate to the inflow and outflow of cash. As with the profit and loss statement, a cash flow statement is prepared to reflect a specific accounting period, such as monthly, quarterly or annually.

You will need to review these reports regularly, at least monthly, so you always know where you stand financially and can quickly move to correct minor difficulties before they become major financial problems.

Paying Your Vendors

Keeping enough money flowing into a business is a universal concern, but the problem can be especially thorny in an industry that requires the payment of vendor and site deposits often months before an event. Planner Lee J. Howard suggests three strategies for maintaining good cash flow:

1. *Start with plenty of cash reserves.* Make sure that the amount you estimated in Chapter 5 for the first six months of operation is realistic.

2. *Take deposits.* Because you must pay vendor and site deposits and also purchase supplies, you should require deposits from clients upon signing of contracts. Dallas planners Deborah Williams, Kim Quigley, and David Granger require a minimum 50 percent deposit, with the balance to be paid at the time of the event. The deposit for an event contracted with very little lead time may be closer to 75 percent. "You should never be in the business of financing someone's party," says Kim. Some event planners require full payment before the event to safeguard their financial interest, finding that once the event is finished the client has less motivation to pay.

3. *Charge enough for your services.* Make a careful assessment of what you need to charge to turn a healthy profit. Don't low-ball your estimates just to get the job. You'll end up financially frustrated. Remember that controlling costs is easier than trying to predict what your revenue will be. Small expenses add up. For example, why pay extra to have a postal company pick up your packages if you can take them there yourself? Once you look for additional ways to save money, you'll find them. And Benjamin Franklin was right: "A penny saved is a penny earned."

> **Tip...**
>
> **Smart Tip**
> Whenever possible, save money by bartering services with other business owners. You could provide planning help in exchange for brochure printing services or the creation of signage, to name only a couple of examples.

Pricing Your Services

As planner Lee Howard suggests above, charging enough—but not too much!—for your services is key to ongoing business success. It is important for first-time business owners to, therefore, proceed with caution as they first begin to estimate the cost of holding events.

The goal in pricing a service is to mark up your labor and materials costs sufficiently to cover overhead expenses and generate an acceptable profit.

According to industry expert Dr. Joe Goldblatt, fees are typically determined by three factors:

Beware!
Remember that small expenses add up. You may supply doughnuts and coffee at morning meetings with your staff. This is great for morale and helps to keep your team happy but be sure to include a "doughnut allowance" when you caluclate expenses!

1. *Market segment served.* Social events have a different fee structure than corporate events. In the social events industry, planners typically receive a fee for their services, plus a percentage of some or all vendor fees. The two income streams produce enough revenue for a profit. If you were to break down your event planning fee into an hourly charge, a social planner would, according to industry consultant and author Patty Sachs, make anywhere from $12 to $75 per hour, depending on experience, plus vendor commissions. In the corporate events industry, however, planners typically charge a fee for their services, plus a handling charge for each item they contract. For example, a planner buys flowers from a florist, marks them up (usually 15 percent) and charges that amount to the client. Another possibility is a flat fee, or "project fee," often used when the event is large and the corporation wants to be given a "not to exceed" figure. Whichever method is used, Sachs estimates an hourly rate for corporate planners of between $16 and $150, plus vendor commissions. As these hourly figures imply, profit margins are typically greater for corporate events than they are for social ones.

2. *Geographic location.* Fees are higher in the Northeast, for example, than in the Southeast. This difference reflects the variation in cost of living. In addition, areas of the country that have well-defined on- and off-seasons, such as the Hamptons in New York or Martha's Vineyard, for example, base their prices partly on the season involved.

3. *Experience and reputation of the event planner.* If you are just starting out in the industry, it is reasonable to charge less for your planning services while you gain expertise. A word of caution, though: don't charge too little just to get the job. Although clients shop around for the best price, a planner who comes in too low with an estimate may be as off-putting as a planner who comes in too high. Your client may question your ability to throw a top-tier event based on the price you have quoted.

How, you may ask, are the above-mentioned fees-for-service calculated? Event planners we interviewed price their fees-for-service (the total cost to the client) using a "cost-plus" method. They contract out the labor, supplies, and materials involved in producing an event and charge their clients about 10 percent to 20 percent of the total cost of the event, with 15 percent being a rough average.

A word of caution concerning this method of pricing. Ideally, the percentage you charge above cost should provide you with a sufficient amount to cover that event's share of your overhead, as well as produce a profit. Overhead comprises all the nonlabor, indirect expenses required to operate your business. In general, overhead will be anywhere between 4 percent and 6 percent of the total price of the event. Your actual overhead expenses may vary depending on your own market conditions. Should your overhead expenses be too high, you will have to raise your commission to maintain sufficient profit. By raising your commission, you could become less competitive. It's a good idea to closely control your overhead expenses so they don't become too high relative to the price of the event.

> **Bright Idea**
> Another way to make sure your business doesn't suffer from a lack of cash is to sell gift certificates toward your planning services. Satisfied customers might buy them, and they are an excellent way to introduce others to your services. Furthermore, gift certificates are money in the bank because people often wait months before cashing them in. Consider, too, if you live in an area with very specific on- and off-seasons, offering $500 gift certificates during the off-season for $450. In this way, you will still keep money flowing into your business during the off-season.

When you consider what percent of the total event to charge a client, examine your role in planning the event. Planner Joyce Barnes-Wolff notes that the rule in the industry is to charge, on average, a commission of between 10 percent and 15 percent, depending on what the event involves. She evaluates the amount of her time and energy spent on the event. "My Rolodex is worth something, but if my role is simply picking up the phone and making calls and showing up for an event, I don't think it rates that kind of coordination fee." But if the event is complicated and creativity is what matters, then 10 percent to 15 percent is "very fair," she says.

Industry markups vary widely, ranging from 100 percent and up. Markup rates depend mostly on overhead costs, but the health of the economy also affects them. In troubled economic times, markups (and therefore profit margins) will be lower.

Maintaining Cash Flow

Along with opening your business with adequate cash reserves, requiring deposits, and charging appropriately for your services, there are several other ways of ensuring good cash flow for your business:

▲

- *Pay your company's bills on time, but do not pay early.* Keep your money in the bank as long as possible. The single exception to this rule applies if you have negotiated vendor discounts for early payment (see Chapter 6). Keep files for bills due in 10 days, 20 days, 30 days, etc. Each Monday, pay the bills due in 10 days. Then, transfer the bills due in 20 days to the bills due in 10 days folder, the bills due in 30 days to the due in 20 days folder, etc. This system of files will ensure that your bills are paid on time—thus obviating any possible late fees—but not too early which would take money out of interest-bearing accounts of your own.

- *Negotiate the latest possible payment of the balance of vendor bills.* Often vendors will give you 30 days after the event in which to pay, especially if you have a good working relationship with them. This means if you get paid on the day of the event, you have 30 days of "free money" before you have to pay your vendors. And if the client is slow in paying, you have a cushion.

- *Make sure your invoices are clear, accurate, and timely.* Being timely means sending your invoices as soon as you sign a contract or complete an event. The difficulty of collecting an account increases in direct proportion to its age. *Always itemize invoices so clients know exactly what they are paying for.*

- *Keep inventory and supplies to a minimum.* According to industry expert and author Robin A. Kring, excessive overhead and inventory costs can seriously affect cash flow.

Adding Up the Costs for an Event

As we mentioned in the research section in Chapter 3, you have to know exactly what your clients want and what they can spend to achieve it before you can begin planning an event. Then you estimate how much it will cost to contract for labor and supplies, add your commission to this sum, and present the total fee for services to the client as an estimate. Make sure you have filled out the Event Design Worksheet starting on page 40. Those client needs will dictate what particular expenses you (and ultimately the client) will incur for that event. Below are some possible per-event expenses:

- *Site rental.* Depending on the event, site rental fees can be considerable, nonexistent, or anywhere in between. This is an opportunity for you to save money for a client on a tight budget. Perhaps a client wants a scenic and sunny summer barbecue. A site at a public beach can often be reserved for practically nothing while tony beach-side clubs often command premium prices.

- *Vendors.* This category could include a caterer, bartender, decorator, florist, photographer, entertainer, videographer, or any of the vendors discussed in Chapter 6.

- *Supplies.* Any supplies not provided by vendors or by the client will need to be purchased by your company. These items can include anything from food to potted trees to table candles.

- *Equipment rental.* You may need to rent audiovisual or lighting equipment.
- *Licenses and permits.* As mentioned in Chapter 4, some types of events require special permits or licenses (e.g., Fire Marshall's permit or a license to use a musical score).
- *Transportation and parking.* If the event requires you or your staff to travel or requires the provision of transport for attendees or speakers, there may be significant transportation costs involved. These can include anything from airfare to car mileage and gasoline allowances.

> **Tip...**
>
> **Smart Tip**
>
> As an additional way to beef up your cash flow, consider requiring clients to pay your bill in three installments rather than two. The first is the deposit, the second is a progress payment, and the third is due at the event itself. Note that if you do this, you will still probably want to have clients pay a deposit of close to 50 percent.

- *Service fees and gratuities.* Hiring temporary help (e.g., servers) for the event can be costly.
- *Speakers' fees.* Conferences and other educational or commemorative events often involve speakers.
- *Publicity and invitations.* Getting the word out can be expensive. A large event may be heavily advertised, but even smaller events might entail the use of fliers. Invitations are also frequently necessary. In this age of e-mail, invitations, especially for corporate events, are often sent via e-mail, a budget-conscious choice.
- *Mailing and shipping.* If you are mailing out invitations or fliers, don't forget this expense. Some event planners even ship flowers.
- *Photocopying and preparation of registration materials.* Any handouts for attendees or photocopying of fliers falls under this category.
- *Research and evaluations.* Depending on the nature of your inquiries and whether clients will benefit from them, you may not want to charge clients for these expenditures.
- *Signage.* Any signs or banners designed for the event should be figured into your per-event expenses. As Cheryl Hagner of Wesleyan University says, don't skimp on this. "Signage is essential to a successful event. There must be good flow and signage helps to create this."

Once you know your client's needs and which of the above expenses you will incur in planning the event, you can prepare an estimate of the event cost and of the fee-for-service. First, find out the going rate by contacting three of each kind of vendor you will need. Do the same for suppliers. Don't forget that price is not everything; consider the quality offered. As the saying goes, "you get what you pay for." So, the inexpensive disc jockey might be the guy to tarnish your event, showing up for a black-tie event in his blue jeans.

Finally, calculate the costs for each category listed (and any others that might arise), add them up, and add a small amount for unforeseen expenses (you be the judge of how much, depending on the size of the event).

When you give an estimate to a client, you may want to present it in the form of an itemized list. Show each vendor or supplier separately, perhaps with a brief description of the services he or she is to provide, and list the price of each service. This strategy is helpful, among other things, for reminding clients that your company will receive only a small fraction of the total fee for services. Add all event expenses together, then figure your commission as a percentage of this event cost.

Suppose you are presenting your estimate for an event that costs $6,945 to produce. Let's

> ## Smart Tip
>
> Although you should strive for an accurate estimate, you may find that your final total differs from the initial estimate. For this reason, you should make it clear to your clients that your estimate of the total event cost is just that—an estimate. Make sure that this fact is stated clearly in your contract. The contract should also specify that the client is responsible for any additional charges. Ensuring that you do not exceed your estimate by an unreasonable amount is an important part of your responsibility to your client.

also assume that you charge a commission of 15 percent, an industry average. After itemizing the event costs, you would add in your commission in this manner:

Event Cost (E): $6,945

Commission (C): (15% of $6,945) =

.15 × 6,945 = $1,042

Finally, add the event cost and your commission to produce the fee-for-service (S). This figure represents the final cost to the client.

Fee-for-Service (S) = Event cost + Commission =

$6,945 + $1,042 = $7,987

So the final cost to the client is $7,987.

Calculating When Your Business Will Break Even

We have cautioned you to make sure you have a substantial amount of operating capital, enough to last until you reach the break-even point. How, you may ask, do you calculate a break-even point for an event planning business? The following is a detailed example of such an analysis:

- *Determine your monthly fixed costs.* Fixed costs (F) are those that do not change, no matter how many events you plan (e.g., rent, utilities). You completed a worksheet of these costs on page 70 in Chapter 5. For the purpose of this break-even example, let's assume that you have monthly fixed costs of $1,910. So F = $1,910.

- *Determine your variable costs.* Variable costs are the costs of putting on the event you produce (e.g., hiring vendors, renting a site). Variable costs combine to produce the "event cost" (E). In this case, E = $6,945.

- *Figure out the fee for service (S).* We just did this in the pricing example. We used an average rate of 15 percent, multiplied it by the event cost (E), and produced a commission (C) of $1,042. We then added the commission to the event cost to produce the fee for service. S = $7,987.

- *Now use the break-even equation.* Break-even = F divided by C: In this equation, F = fixed expenses and C = commission. Inputting our data from the example above, we find: Break-even = $1,910 divided by $1,042 = 1.8 events.

According to this break-even analysis, you will need to plan about two $8,000 events per month to pay all expenses and start making a profit.

> ### Beware!
> You must keep records to determine your tax liabilities. Regardless of the type of bookkeeping system you use, your records must be permanent, accurate, and complete, and they must clearly establish income, deductions, credits, employee information, and anything else specified by federal, state, and local regulations. You must keep complete and separate records for each business.

You and Your Taxes

Managing your finances includes keeping a careful eye on your tax liabilities. These include:

- *Sales taxes.* Sales taxes are levied by many cities and states at varying rates. Most provide specific exemptions for certain classes of merchandise or particular groups of customers. Service businesses are often exempt altogether. Contact your state and/or local revenue offices for information on the law in your area so you can adapt your bookkeeping to the appropriate requirements. Many of the entrepreneurs we spoke to have resale tax ID numbers for their companies. This number entitles a business to buy merchandise (e.g., flowers) tax-free and charge clients the sales tax.

- *Personal income taxes.* If you are a sole proprietor or partner, you will not receive a salary like an employee. Therefore, no income tax will be withheld from the money you take out of your business for personal use. Instead, you must estimate your personal tax liability and pay it in quarterly installments.

- *Corporate income taxes*. If your business is organized as a corporation, you must pay taxes on all profits.

In addition to paying your own taxes, as a business owner and employer you will be responsible for collecting employee state and federal taxes and remitting them to the proper agencies. If you are a sole proprietor and plan to hire an employee, call the IRS at (800) TAX-FORM or access the information at www.irs.gov. Ask for a copy of Form SS-4. Also call your state tax agency.

If you are like most event planners, you will hire some individuals as independent contrac-

> **Tip...**
>
> ## Smart Tip
> All withheld income tax is treated as if spread equally over the calendar year, even when a disproportionately large amount is withheld in December. If you are required to make estimated tax payments, you should pay special attention to other techniques that may be beneficial, especially if your income is irregular or seasonal.

tors (e.g., vendors). According to the IRS definition, independent contractors are individuals who perform services for more than one firm, determine how the work is to be done, use their own tools, hire and pay their own employees, and work for a fee rather than a salary. If you hire independent contractors, you have to file an annual information return (Form 1099—Miscellaneous) to report payments totaling $600 or

Working It Out

Good tax planning not only minimizes your taxes, but provides more money for your business. As an entrepreneur, you should view tax savings as a potential source of working capital. There are a few important rules to follow in your tax planning:

○ Don't incur an additional expense solely for the sake of getting an extra deduction. This strategy is not cost-effective.

○ Immediately deferring taxes allows you to use your money interest-free before paying it to the government. Interest rates may justify deferring taxes, though doing so may cost you more taxes in a later year.

○ If possible, claim income in the most advantageous year. If, as you begin your business, you are employed by someone else and expect to receive a year-end bonus or other additional compensation, you may want to defer receipt until the forthcoming year, especially if you will be in a lower tax bracket at that time (e.g., perhaps quitting your job to devote full time to your business).

more made to any individual in the course of trade or business during the calendar year. If you do not file this form, you will be subject to penalties. Be sure your records list the name, address, and Social Security number of every independent contractor you hired, along with pertinent dates and the amounts paid to each person. Every payment should be supported by an invoice from the contractor. Be warned also that if the IRS feels a worker whom you treated as a contractor should have been treated as an employee, you will be liable for payroll taxes that should have been withheld and paid, plus penalties and interest.

Deducting Expenses

As an event planner, you may be able to deduct for the following types of expenses:

- *Home office.* You can deduct for all normal office expenses plus interest, taxes, insurance, and depreciation on the portion of your home that you use exclusively for business. To deduct, however, you must satisfy the following four usage criteria: Exclusive use (the space is not used for anything else), regular use (occasional use doesn't qualify), business use (you must conduct business, see clients, etc., in that space), and administrative use (you must handle administrative tasks at that location). Be aware that the IRS audits a high percentage of taxpayers with home offices.

- *Computers.* A home computer used exclusively for business may qualify for appropriate business deductions or credits.

- *Automobiles.* Depending on which method you use, you may deduct for mileage or for mileage plus depreciation, garage rent, insurance, and repairs, among other expenses.

- *Travel.* You must stay overnight on business to claim deductions on air, bus, or auto fares, hotel bills, and incidentals like dry cleaning and gratuities.

- *Entertainment.* You can deduct 50 percent of your expenses, but you must maintain records of the following: amount of expenditure; date of expenditure; name, address and type of entertainment; occupation of the person entertained; reason for entertainment; and the nature of the business discussion that took place (general goodwill is not accepted by the IRS). Rules for deductions change frequently. You can also look online at www.irs.gov for tax updates.

Beware!
Make sure you do not make a mistake about what is tax-deductible. Penalty rates are high. Check with your accountant to be sure your deductions are legitimate. An IRS audit is not only inconvenient, it could be costly.

- *Conferences and seminars.* The cost of the actual seminar is deductible, but deductions are no longer permitted for many of the expenses (e.g. food, lodging) incurred in connection with a conference, convention, or seminar.
- *Dues and subscriptions.* You may deduct these as long as they pertain to your field of business.

With proper management of your company's financial resources, you can greatly increase the probability that your business will succeed. In the next chapter, we'll discuss more ways you can ensure the success of your business.

Onward and
Upward

This chapter has two topics: failure and success. Because we want to quickly move on to the more cheerful, optimistic topic, we'll first take a swift pass at ways to avoid failure.

Keep Your Business Healthy

Event Planning News

According to Cheryl Hagner, Director of University Events and Scheduling at Wesleyan University, the most important skill an event planner must possess is the ability to put out fires, both literal and figurative. Hagner oversees 9,000 events annually and problems can and do arrive. She says, though, that her clients remain satisfied as long as she is able to think creatively and resolve the problem quickly.

We're guessing that what you've read in earlier chapters has already given you an idea of the potential glitches of event planning. If you want to give yourself a little test, put down this book, make a list, and then compare it with ours. (If you feel your test-taking days are over, no problem. Just read on.) Here are some of the pitfalls specific to the event planning industry:

- *Misunderstanding your client's requirements.* If your client wants a conservative business meeting and you deliver a Roaring Twenties theme party, you're in trouble. Although this is an extreme example, remember that you need to know all your client's requirements in detail before you can arrange a successful event. As Cheryl Hagner points out, this is a particular skill. "Event planners absolutely have to be good listeners, and to hear what is said *between the lines.*"

- *Poor choice of vendors or site.* Do your homework. Contract with reliable, reputable vendors who can meet your client's needs exactly. If your caterer serves a terrible meal, it's the caterer's fault that he or she can't cook. However, you're the one who made the hiring decision, so you'll take the blame. The buck stops with you. Be sure you can count on your vendors. *Vet vendors carefully.*

- *Lack of coordination between you and your team.* This is a related pitfall. Make sure you have a cooperative, "well-oiled" team (employees, vendors, and temporary staff) around you, and that everyone understands their respective roles in the production of the event. You know the adage—you're only as good as your weakest link. Avoid weak links!

- *Inaccurate estimates.* Your estimates should be as accurate as possible. If events go far over budget, your clients may end up having to pay more money than they can afford. If, on the other hand, you consistently come in at or below your estimates, you will probably have satisfied clients who will gladly recommend you to others. Clients may feel "taken to the cleaners" if you come in substantially higher than you originally estimated.

- *Inadequate control of costs.* Take every reasonable opportunity to save. Pay attention to where money goes. Compare costs and choose wisely.

- *Poor cash flow*. In Chapter 8 we discussed ways to avoid this problem. One of the most effective is to require client deposits.

- *Inadequate insurance*. Make sure that you carry enough insurance to protect yourself in case anything goes wrong at an event. The planners that we spoke to carry about $1 million of liability insurance. If you don't have enough of the proper insurance, and if you're involved in a lawsuit, you could end up in bankruptcy.

- *Poor customer service*. Much of what we covered in Chapter 7 can be encapsulated

Smart Tip

If you feel your business is floundering, don't wait to ask for assistance. The Small Business Association reports that too many small business owners ignore financial red flags and don't look for help until it is too late to save their companies. Check with the SBA (www.sba.org) for advice and guidance.

into one piece of advice: Make the event right. This is a golden rule in the event planning industry. Nancy Lavin, a regional vice president of an asset management firm, has hired event planners for hundreds of events, ranging from dinners at big-name steak houses to high-touch events at professional sporting events. For her, the deal breaker is poor service. "I understand if problems arise at big events. Things happen. However, the complete deal breaker is poor service. If my client has to wait, then I am not using that event planner again. That sounds tough, but the people I entertain want to be wowed—impressive location, great attentive staff, awesome food."

So how did you do? Now that you know some of the problems that can undermine an event planning business, be alert for any danger signs. If you react quickly enough, you can prevent financial disaster from striking. Ideally, of course, you will not merely react to threats, but instead anticipate changes, whether in the event planning field itself, in your clients' demands, or in the financial state of your business.

When Bad Things Happen to Good Event Planners

Even the best event planners face pot holes at some events. It's the nature of the business. It is important to plan for possible large-impact scenarios like inclement weather or security-related emergencies. Before the event, take a few moments to think through "what-ifs" and plan crisis management strategies with your staff. Make sure you know—and have readily available—the facility's emergency and security procedures. Also make sure personnel trained in CPR and other emergency procedures are present at the event.

Occasionally, in spite of your best efforts and meticulous planning, something goes wrong during an event. At that point, your biggest challenge may be to remain calm in the crisis and to think on your feet. However, if you're imagining disaster lurking around every corner, out of your control and waiting to trip you up, take heart. Because, in fact, much of effective troubleshooting is within your control and consists simply of making adequate preparations. In other words, in many cases good troubleshooting is proactive rather than reactive. Try to anticipate where problems might arise and plan for them. This strategy can be as simple as having backups for resources that are critical to an event's success.

Planner Martin Van Keken's firm produced a huge event on closing night of the Royal Ballet in Vancouver, British Columbia. Held outside at the Queen Elizabeth Theatre, the event's decor featured a spectacular English garden. Foreign dignitaries, including Margaret Thatcher and Princess Margaret, were in attendance. The evening event required a generator to supply power, and just before the guests were to enter the tented area, the generator failed. "It could not have happened at a worse moment," says Van Keken. Fortunately, they had a backup generator, although hooking it up took time. "A very long five or ten minutes" after the guests entered the tented area, the lights came on, revealing the English garden decor. And the guests applauded. "They all thought it was choreographed that way," says Martin. His story has a happy ending, but only because his company had the vital backup system.

Sometimes good troubleshooting involves persistence and a refusal to give up. Atlanta planner Lee J. Howard tells a story of a power failure in a building during one of his company's events. The building manager, who was responsible for backup power, said it wasn't working either and that there was no way to get help until Monday. "Meanwhile, we had a live band and 200 dancers on the floor." After examining the possibilities, they decided to try all the electrical outlets close to the stage. One in the men's room worked, and they had amplified music back on within 15 minutes. "Although it was July and there was no AC or power for anything else, the party carried on successfully," he says. "The bottom line is, we took responsibility and didn't give up."

Beware!

With event planning, you don't have a second chance. If an event goes wrong, you can't tell the client to come back the next night. Keep yourself sane, however, by remembering that "There's no such thing as the perfect event," as Martin Van Keken puts it. Some event elements will be beyond your control. Be flexible and ready to think on your feet. Finally, don't be defensive with your client. Be professional and take responsibility. Perhaps, you need to negotiate a discount if the event was severely disrupted. Or, perhaps, you can offer a discount on a future service.

There's a Mouse in the House

For Sue Meyer, founder of Susan K. Meyer Consulting, the dinner for a high-powered group of business people started off well.

We were at a dinner event at which several of our partners were coming in to a very nice restaurant—one of the area's top places. We were seated at a table for eight and were served our salads. Then I noticed all of this commotion to the right of me. It was a formal dinner so I didn't want to jump up and interfere. The manager approached me and, shaking his head, said, 'It's no big deal. I'll tell you later.'

The waiter came and a round of free drinks came. I still had no clue. I have worked many times with the manager of this restaurant so knew that if it were a big problem he would approach me. When he didn't, I knew everything was fine and the partners at the table went on after the commotion to enjoy their meal.

The next day, I went to a workshop—all part of this same meeting. And what do I hear? 'Thanks for the extra protein at dinner.' I came to find out that the partner at the end of the table had been served grilled heart of romaine—but inside the heart was a grey field mouse the size of a thumb! He noticed some wilting and was poking around with his fork. He was very nice about it, not making a big scene. Since the manager didn't tell me, I was a goof and shook the chef's hand—I looked like a fool. This chef fed my client a mouse!

The next day, an invoice was shot over to my office from the restaurant. There was no discount, no 'sorry about the mouse,' no nothing! So, I called, and initially the manager was resistant to doing anything! I couldn't believe it—I had scheduled many high-end dinners at this restaurant.

After some discussion he agreed to cancel the $5,000 bill and to donate to a community cause—I asked him to go this extra step. Of course, I haven't gone back.

Meyer used her negotiating skills to save her client $5,000. She also learned, the hard way, that the manager she trusted was not so trustworthy. He should have alerted her to the situation immediately. Instead, apparently, he hoped and planned that she would never be told about this mysterious mouse business.

Remember the best way to deal with unforeseen circumstances you cannot control is to remain as flexible as possible and be willing to try new strategies.

Recipe for Success

Besides being a good troubleshooter, what strategies can you adopt to give your event planning business the best possible chance for success? The planners and industry experts we interviewed provided the following advice:

Stay calm, advises Cheryl Hagner. "It sounds like simple advice, but if event planners are able to stay calm—even when the kitchen has been accidentally set ablaze by the caterer, then your client will feel calm and reassured, too."

Create good energy at every event, says Lauren Polastri. Again, sounds simple, but Polastri points out that "you get what you give. Always try to establish a friendly relationship. It's a much nicer way to do business.

- *Acquire professional training.* Says industry expert Dr. Joe Goldblatt, "The shortest route between exploring and succeeding in this profession is affiliation with a well-known school or university." Industry expert John Daly also recommends formal training. Community colleges and continuing education programs also offer courses valuable to event planners.

- *Provide the service you say you will.* Use written contracts and stick to them. "And keep good records," suggests New York planner Jaclyn Bernstein.

- *Concentrate on the type of planning you do best.* "Don't try to do it all," advises industry expert and author Robin A. Kring.

- *Create a reliable team around you.* All planners mentioned the importance of staffing and vendor choices. "You design an event on paper," says Martin Van Keken. "Then you rely on other people."

- *Walk through the event.* Event planner Joyce Barnes-Wolff always does a mental walk-through: "In my mind I'm there. Do I have enough time? Are the press kits there?"

Event planning is exciting and dynamic but it is challenging. As Susan Meyer puts it, "people gravely underestimate what it takes to throw an event." Keep you mind open to continued education and remember that event planning involves a learning curve. The more events you plan, the more confident and accomplished you will become.

- *"Try to be one step ahead,"* suggests Martin Van Keken. "Getting upset doesn't help," he adds.

- *Expect the unexpected.* Many event planners mentioned this one. "There's always something that will go differently than planned," says Van Keken. Not necessarily wrong, he stresses, but differently. "You've got to be ready for that."

- *Be ready with Plan B.* This is closely related to the last piece of advice. "I never do an outdoor event without a rain plan," says Barnes-Wolff.

An Educational Experience

If you decide to get formal training in special events, there are several avenues you can explore. Consider courses in event management through a program such as the one at George Washington University in Washington, DC. Goldblatt, founder of the program, says that it offers both a master's degree and a certificate program. Certification requires a minimum of seven courses and takes two years to complete. Courses are offered on campus, in five other cities, and through distance learning (i.e., via the internet). For more information, consult the program's Web site at www.gwu.edu.

The International Special Events Society (ISES) Conference for Professional Development (CPD) is a series of professional seminars focusing on the latest trends and developments in the special events industry. Offered through ISES, this conference offers both educational and networking opportunities.

As previously mentioned, The Special Event also offers you a chance to learn as you network. Held annually in January, this prestigious industry trade show is put on by Primedia Business Magazine & Media Inc., which also publishes *Special Events* magazine. For contact information on any of these sources, consult the Appendix.

- *Make your clients happy.* As we have stated, this is a golden rule in event planning. "In this industry there is no right or wrong except to make the client happy," says Granger. Doing the work and getting it right is what matters, agrees Bernstein.

Looking Ahead

Developing a strong customer base, paying close attention to clients' needs, finding a niche, and coping with a changing economy are all proven ways to keep a business successful and out of financial difficulty. Remember, periodically ask yourself the following questions:

- Have I carefully analyzed the demand for my services, monitored the marketplace, and adjusted to changing conditions?
- Have I found a niche that provides me with enough events to plan, without involving too wide a range?
- Do I have an accurate and realistic amount of cash reserves?

▲

- Do I have a business plan and mission statement?
- Are my services priced accurately?
- Have I kept my overhead costs to an absolute minimum?
- Have I created a good team, with well-chosen staff and vendors?
- Does my company provide the kind of customer service that keeps clients coming back?
- Do I market my company effectively?

If you answered "yes" to all these questions, congratulations! Your company has an excellent chance of success. If you had any "no" answers, these are the areas that need work. And identifying these areas puts you in a good position to make the corrections that will create a thriving business.

Event planning is a "happy" industry. You have chosen a field that will allow you to create wonderful memories for many people. If you do just that, success will follow. So go out there and have fun!

And celebrate!

Appendix
Event Planning Resources

These listings are suggestions for finding event planning resources, from professional associations to useful books, educational opportunities, recommended magazines and journals, and trend-tracking advice.

These sources, though, are only the beginning. They are by no means the only sources available to you, nor can any claim total authority. Event planning is a volatile field, and businesses tend to move, change, fold, and expand. It's up to you to do your homework. Get out and start asking questions.

Make full use of the internet. Because of the fast-changing nature of the event-planning field, the web offers invaluable resources. So, let your fingers do the walking, on your computer keyboard, to find additional resources.

Associations

ASAE and *The Center for Association Leadership*, 1575 I St. NW, Washington, DC 20005-1103, (202) 371-0940, www.asaecenter.org

Convention Industry Council, 1620 I St. NW, Washington, DC 20006, (202) 429-8634, www.conventionindustry.org

▲

Event Planners Association, 860-380-3EPA, www.eventplannersassociation.com

International Association of Convention & Visitors Bureaus, 2025 M St. NW, #500, Washington, DC 20036, (202) 296-7888, www.iacvb.org

International Festivals & Events Association, 2601 Eastover Terrace, Boise, ID 83706, (208) 433-0950, www.ifea.com

International Special Events Society, 401 N. Michigan Ave., Chicago, IL 60611, (800) 688-4737, www.ises.com

Meeting Professionals International, 3030 LBJ Fwy., #1700, Dallas, TX 75234, (972) 702-3000, www.mpiweb.org

National Association of Catering Executives, (410) 290-5410, www.nace.net

Professional Convention Management Association, 2301 S. Lake Shore Dr., #1001, Chicago, IL 60616-1419, (312) 423-7262, www.pcma.org

Books

This list is literally the tip of the book iceberg in terms of books which might be useful to you. If your specialization is bar and bat mitzvahs, for instance, you will want to research additional titles applying directly to your specialization. The books listed here are more general in nature.

Your local library is a wonderful resource. Also, be sure to check a book's copyright. A book published in the early 1990's, for instance, will lack relevance with regard to the event planning business of today.

Art of the Event, James Monroe and Robert Kates, John Wiley & Sons, Inc. (2005)

The Business of Event Planning: Behind-the-Scenes Secrets of Successful Special Events, Judy Allen, John Wiley & Sons Inc. (2002)

The Complete Guide to Successful Event Planning, Shannon Kilkenny, Atlantic Publishing (2007)

The Complete Idiot's Guide to Event Planning, Robin Craven and Lynn Johnson Golabowski, Alpha Books (2006)

Event Planning Guide for Charity and Not-for-Profit Organizations, Harry Von Bommel, Media Futures Institute (2006)

Event Planning: The Ultimate Guide to Successful Meetings, Corporate Events, Fundraising Galas, Conferences, Conventions, Incentives and Other Special Events, Judy Allen, John Wiley & Sons (2000)

Fab Job Guide to Becoming an Event Planner, Jan Riddell, Carol Palmatier, Peter Gallanis, Fabjob (2006)

Pocket Idiot's Guide to Choosing a Caterer, Phyllis Cambria and Patty Sachs, Alpha (2004)

Special Events: Event Leadership for a New World, Dr. Joe Goldblatt, John Wiley & Sons Inc. (2004)

Educational Opportunities

Alan Shawn Feinstein Graduate School, offers the first MBA concentration in Event Leadership, www.jwu.edu

Convention Industry Council, offers training to become a Certified Meeting Professional, www.conventionindustry.org

The George Washington University International Institute of Tourism Studies offers both a master's degree and a certificate program in event management, www.gwu.edu

International Special Events Society, provides certification as a Certified Special Events Professional, www.ises.com

Event Planning Software

There are hundreds of types of event planning software, ranging from inexpensive and basic packages to software developed for planning and managing large-scale conventions and trade shows. This software ranges in price from $100 to thousands of dollars. As your company grows, you will need to determine the types of software you will need.

Meeting Professionals International for a detailed look at the characteristics of more than 170 types of meeting software, www.mpiweb.org

Industry Experts

John Daly Jr., CSEP, John Daly Inc., www.jdalyinc.com

Dr. Joe Goldblatt, CSEP, Dean, Alan Shawn Feinstein Graduate School, Johnson & Wales University, www.jwu.edu

Patty Sachs, author and presenter (with Phyllis Cambria) of several event planning books, www.partyplansplus.com

Magazines and Publications

This listing primarily includes magazines and journals geared toward those in the event planning trade. Remember, any event planner worth her salt also reads consumer magazines to keep on top of trends. For instance, many event planners mentioned *Martha Stewart Living* as a source for current food, floral, and decorating information.

Event Solutions Magazine, www.event-solutions.com

The Meeting Professional, www.mpiweb.org

Meetings & Conventions, www.meetings-conventions.com

Special Events Magazine, www.specialevents.com

Successful Meetings, www.vnusub.com

Tradeshow Week, www.tradeshowweek.com

Travel Weekly, www.travelweekly.com

Web Sites of Interest to Event Planners

These are some of our favorite web sites. As you surf the internet, you will find your own favorites, as well.

www.alltimefavorites.com (All Time Favorites Inc.), a good site for searching for vendors and getting proposals.

www.bizbash.com (BizBash.com), a trendy site, featuring lots of ideas for events.

www.conworld.net (Conworld.net), contains, among other things, a list of event planning software.

www.dmoz.org (Open Directory Project), the hospitality software section in the business area features a long list of software sites for event planning.

www.event-planner.com (Event Planner), provides many useful resources.

www.eventplanner.com (EventPlanner.com), more resources.

www.eventplanning.net (The Event Planning Network), find suppliers, planning tips, chat and discussion areas, etc.

www.event-plans.com (Event Plans), lists many event planning themes and trends.

www.expoworld.net (Sponsored by Las Vegas Convention and Visitors Authority), offers many event sites, publications, directories, and articles.

www.ezeventplanner.com (EZEventPlanner), use this site to help you plan your entire event.

www.ises.com (International Special Events Society), an association of more than 4,000 special events professionals; web site features information on joining ISES, a forum for networking with event planners and others in the special events industry, an online copy of ISES' code of ethics, information on local chapters, and more.

www.meetings-conventions.com (Meetings & Conventions Online), contains news and feature stories from the latest issue of *Meetings & Conventions* magazine, an events calendar, directory of previously published articles (which have to be ordered separately), plus links to conventions and visitors bureaus throughout the United States.

www.mpiweb.org (Meeting Professionals International), an organization of meeting planners for the corporate market (some of whom are independent planners) supports this web site consisting mainly of membership information and benefits; you'll also find a database of MPI suppliers, an online version of its bookstore catalog, and local chapter information.

www.seatingarrangement.com (SeatingArrangement), plan your seating using information from this site.

www.specialeventsite.com (SpecialEventSite), search for many different types of sites.

Successful Event Planners

Designs Behind the Scenes Inc., Deborah K. Williams, Kim I. Quigley, David Granger, 2809 Canton St., Dallas, TX 75226, (214) 747-1904, www.dbtsinc.com

Empire Force Events Inc., Jaclyn Bernstein, www.empireforce.com

JBW Productions, Joyce Barnes-Wolff, www.jbwProductions.com

Lee J. Howard Entertainment Inc., Lee J. Howard, www.leehowardentertainment.com

MVKA Productions, Martin Van Keken, www.mvka.com

The Other Woman, Lauren Polastri, 203-481-1882

Glossary

Actualization: an accounting of an event planning business's expenditures (both time and money) in producing an event.

American Society of Association Executives (ASAE): an organization for association executives.

Blog: an online journal or newsletter, usually with more than one author.

Bond: an insurance contract used by service companies as a guarantee that they have the necessary ability and financial backing to meet their obligations.

Break-even point: the point at which your company neither makes nor loses money.

Caterer: a company retained to provide food (and usually beverages, too) for an event.

Contingency plan: a written plan that is prepared in advance to address possible emergencies.

Chat room: on the internet, an electronic gathering place for people who share special interests, where they exchange ideas, information, and brainstorm.

▲

Contractor: an individual or a company under contract to provide goods or services.

Convention and visitors bureau: nonprofit organization that provides products and services to planners.

Copyright: a form of protection used to safeguard original literary works, performing arts, sound recordings, and visual arts.

Corporate planner: an individual who plans meetings for companies.

Corporation: a separate legal entity distinct from its owners.

Demongraphics: the primary characteristics of your target audience, such as age, gender, ethnic background, income level, education level, and home ownership.

Destination management company (DMC): a business that handles entertainment for a group of individuals (often conference or meeting attendees) from out of town.

Doing Business As (DBA): a reference to your legal designation once you have selected a business name different from your own and registered it with the local or state government.

Domain name: the address of an internet network.

Evaluation: written feedback about an event from attendees or other parties.

Home page: the gateway to your internet web site.

High-touch: A term referring to events that require a high degree of care and handling.

Indemnification: a legal term meaning one party agrees to protect the other party from liability or damages related to an event.

International Special Events Society (ISES): the largest association for special events professionals.

Invoice: a document that indicates costs for goods or services owed by one individual or company to another.

Liability: the legal responsibility for an act, especially as pertaining to insurance risks.

Limited Liability Corporation (LLC): a business structure combining the tax structure of a partnership yet protecting the owner from personal liability.

Logo: a symbol used to identify or brand your business.

Markup: the amount added to the cost of goods or services to produce the desired profit.

Meeting professional: an individual who plans and provides services for meetings, conferences, etc.

Meeting Professionals International (MPI): the largest association for meeting professionals.

Newsletter: a marketing piece that offers short, newsy pieces about your business. Newsletters may be sent through regular mail or e-mail.

Partnership: a business owned equally by two or more persons.

Proposal: a document outlining what a business will do for a client and the price at which it will be done.

Relational database: a set of data structured so that information can be accessed across different databases.

Site: the location for an event.

Sole proprietor: a company owned by one person.

Supplier: the individual or company that sells goods or services to another company; term often used synonymously with "vendor."

Target market: the section of the market, or group of people, to whom a company hopes to sell its product.

Telemarketing: Using the phone to generate new sales or leads.

Vendor: the company retained by an event planner to handle one or more aspects of an event; term sometimes used synonymously with "supplier."

Vendor agreement: a legal contract between event planner and vendor.

Venue: a site for an event.

Web site: a group of related documents posted on the internet, usually accessed through a home page.

Index